CATALOGUE

OF THE

BRAZILIAN SECTION.

PHILADELPHIA

INTERNATIONAL EXHIBITION,

1876.

Press of Hallowell & Co.,
121 South Third St., Philadelphia.

COMMITTEE

REPRESENTING

THE EMPIRE OF BRAZIL

AT THE

PHILADELPHIA INTERNATIONAL ·EXHIBITION.

PRESIDENT.

ANTONIO PEDRO DE CARVALHO BORGES—Member of the Council of H. M. the Emperor; Officer of the Orders of the Rose and of Christ; Envoy Extraordinary and Minister Plenipotentiary of Brazil, in the United States of North America.

VICE PRESIDENT.

PHILIPPE LOPES NETTO—Member of the Council of H. M. the Emperor; Dignitary of the Order of the Cross; Commander of that of the Rose; decorated with several foreign orders; and Batchelor in juridical and social sciences.

SECRETARY.

DR. JOAO MARTINS DA SILVA COUTINHO—Commander of the Order of the Rose; Chevalier of the Legion of Honor of France, and of that of Izabel the Catholic of Spain; and a Civil Engineer.

MEMBERS.

DR. HERMENEGILDO RODRIGUES DE ALVARENGA.

DR. JOSE DE SALDANHA DA GAMA—Commander of the Orders of the Rose, of Conceição de Nossa Senhora de Villa Viçosa of Portugal, of Francis Joseph of Austria; Officer of that of the Crown of Italy, and Professor of Botany at the Polytechnic School.

DR. NICOLAU JOAQUIM MOREIRA—Commander of the Order of the Rose, Chevalier of that of Christ, Second Vice President of the Societies of Acclimation, Promoter of National Industry, and Propagator of Fine Arts.

DR. PEDRO DIAS GORDILHO PAES LEME—Chevalier of the Orders of Christ, and of the Rose.

DELEGATE FOR THE NAVY.

COMMANDER LUIZ PHILIPPE DE SALDANHA DA GAMA.

STATISTIC INFORMATION.

EMPIRE OF BRAZIL.

STATISTIC INFORMATION.

GEOGRAPHICAL POSITION.

Latitude, 5°, 10′ N. to 33°, 46′, 10″ S.
Longitude, 8°, 21′, 24″ E. to 32° W. of Rio de Janeiro.

Area in square Kilometres,	8,337,218
Population,	12,000,000

PUBLIC REVENUE.

General Income,	$58,888,888.00
Provincial Income,	12,073,000.00
Municipal Income,	2,528,000.00
Absolute General Income,	71,972,672.00
General Expenditure,	67,234,620.00

RAILROADS.

22 Lines under traffic,	1,660 Kilometres.
16 Lines in course of construction,	1,362 Kilometres.
Projected lines under survey,	6,531 Kilometres.
Capital Invested,	$102,778,000.00
Capital decreed by government,	$200,000,000.00

ANNUAL SUBSIDIES.

Seacoast and Fluvial lines,	$2,000,000.00
Extention of navigation of Seacoast and Fluvial lines,	24,500 miles.
Railroads,	$5,000,000.00

PUBLIC WORKS.

Annual Expenditures,	$7,000,000.00

INDUSTRIES.

Agriculture,	$71,000,000,000.00
Cattle Raising,	2,000,000,000.00
Manufactures,	300,000,000.00

PUBLIC INSTRUCTION.

Primary and Secondary Schools,	6,000
Number of Pupils,	200,000
Annual Expenditure,	$3,000,000.00
High Schools, Number of Pupils,	4,400
Annual Expenditure,	$1,388,888,00
Public Libraries,	110
Containing volumes,	461,300
Journals,	300
Printing Offices,	320
Scientific Societies,	40
Industrial Societies,	50
Museums,	12

COMMERCIAL MOVEMENT.

Exports,	$158,743,000.00
Imports,	138,172,800.00
Total,	$296,915,800.00

ARMY.

Regular Army in time of peace,	16,000
Regular Army in time of war,	32,000
National Guard,	772,000
National Guard reserve,	125,180

NAVY.

Iron-clad vessels,	15
Wooden vessels,	55
Marines in service,	5,340

ARTICLES OF EXPORT.

Coffee, Cotton, Sugar, Cacáo, Caoutchouc, Hides, Curnauba, Wax, Nuts, Woods, Medicinal Herbs, Tobacco, Cumarù, Urucu, Isinglass, Tapioca, Candied Fruits, Cereals, Matté, Vanilla, Copaiba, Cloves, Piassava, Copal, Feathers, Bones, Hoofs, Horns, Tea, Gold-dust, Diamonds, and Spirits.

CATALOGUE.

MAIN BUILDING.

DEPARTMENT I.
MINING AND METALLURGY.

MAIN BUILDING.

DEPARTMENT I.

MINING AND METALLURGY.

MINERALS, ORES, BUILDING-STONES, AND MINING PRODUCTS.

---o---

CLASS 100.

1. **Commission for the Province of Paraná.** Specimens of IRON MINERALS.
2. **Commission for the Province of S. Paulo.** Specimens of IRON MINERALS.
3. **Ypanema Iron Works.** S. João de Ypanema; Province of S. Paulo. Specimens of IRON MINERALS.
4. **M. J. da Cunha Bettencourt.** Rio Tibagy; Province of Paraná. Collection of MINERALS.
5. **Professor H. Gorceix.** Province of Minas Geraes. Collection of ROCKS and MINERALS.
6. **Commission General for the National Exhibitions.** Rio de Janeiro. Specimens of MINERALS from S. Paulo.
   Specimens of MINERALS, Schist and Gneiss, from Minas Geraes.
   Specimens of MINERALS from Matto Grôsso.

7. **National Museum. Rio de Janeiro.** Collection of MINERALS.

8. **J. T. Pereira de Goes. Province of Ceará.** Collection of MINERALS.

9. **J. A. de Lemos. Province of Sergipe.** Collection of MINERALS from the Province of Sergipe.

10. **J. Severo Correia. Province of Paraná.** Specimen of CALCAREOUS ROCKS. Assungy.

11. **M. E. de S. Athayde. Province of Paraná.** Specimens of gold and silver-colored MICA.

12. **J. Severo Correia. Assungy; Province of Paraná.** Specimens of GALENA and of IRON PYRITES, found in Granite.

13. **M. G. de Moraes Rozeira. Palmeira; Province of Paraná.** Specimens of MARTIAL PYRITES.

14. **J. O. Mendes. Province of Paraná.** Specimens of SULPHUR.

15. **J. da Costa Netto. Province of Bahia.** FOSSILS.

CLASS 101.

16. **Commission for the Province of S. Pedro do Sul.** Specimens of COAL.

17. **Baron de Villa Franca. Quissamã; Rio de Janeiro.** Specimens of TURF.

18. **A. R. L. Andrade. Ponta Grossa; Province of Paraná.** Specimens of BITUMINOUS COAL.

19. **Viscount de Barbacena. Rio de Janeiro.** Specimens of COAL from Tubarão; Province of Sancta Catharina.

20. **Commission for the Province of Sancta Catharina.** Specimens of COAL from the Mines of Araranguá.

21. **National Museum. Rio de Janeiro.** Specimens of COAL from different localities.

22. **Commission General for the National Exhibitions.** **Rio de Janeiro.** Specimens of COAL from Rio Grande do Sul.
23. **F. J. A. Lopez & Co. Province of Paraná.** Specimens of BITUMINOUS SCHIST from "Rio Negro."
24. **A. P. S. Carvalho. Province of Paraná.** Specimens of BITUMINOUS SCHIST from Ponta Grossa.
25. **Dr. J. C. da Silva Muricy; Province of Paraná.** Specimens of ANTHRACITE and of BITUMINOUS COAL from "Guarapava." The Exhibitor claims the abundance of these products and their chemical contents, which proportions are:

  Coke, 61.3 per cent.
  Ashes, 2.72 "
  Volatiles, 38.6 "

CLASS 102.

26. **Commission for the Province of Sancta Catharina.** Specimens of MARBLE from Jatajahy.
27. **National Museum. Rio Janeiro.** Specimens of MARBLES from different localities.
28. **Commisson General for the National Exhibitions. Rio de Janeiro.** Specimens of MARBLES from Rio Grande do Sul.
29. **E. Steraux. S. Paulo.** Collection of MARBLES from S. Paulo.

 J. Severo Corréa. Province of Paraná. Specimens of blue-colored SLATES from Assungy.

31. **Dr. A. D. de Leão. Province of Paraná.** Specimens of calcareous SLATES from "Arraial Queimado."
32. **Coritiba Museum. Province of Paraná.** SLATES.
33. **Charles Osternack. Province of Paraná.** VIRGIN LIME.
34. **Baron de Juparanä,** and **Nogueira da Gama. Valença; Province of Rio de Janeiro.** CALCAREOUS SPECIMENS.

35. **Dr. T. Teixeira de Freitas.** Assungy; Province of Paraná. LIME from calcareous stones.

36. **A. Nunes Cardoso.** Antonina; Province of Paraná. LIME from oyster shells.

37. **F. P. de Asevedo Portugal.** Assungy; Province of Paraná. Specimens of calcareous ROCKS.

38. **Commission for S. João d'El Rei; Province of Minas Geraes.** Samples of pulverized PLASTER OF PARIS.

39. **J. S. da Silva Nhorinho.** Campo Largo; Province of Paraná. Specimens of LIME.

40. **Dr. Bento. Itapuã; Province of Bahia.** Samples of common LIME.

41. **L. B. Lendenberg. Cape Frio; Rio de Janeiro.** Samples of LIME.

42. **C. Xavier Rezende. Province of Minas Geraes.** Specimens of STALACTITES.

43. **Commission General for the National Exhibitions. Rio de Janeiro.** STALACTITES and STALAGMITES.

44. **J. Olinto Mendes. Campo Largo; Province of Paranà.** Calcareous STALACTITES.

45. **Dr. A. de Leão. Queimado; Province of Paraná.** Specimens of calcareous STALACTITES.

46. **T. Teixeira de Freitas. Province of Paraná.** Specimens of VIRGIN LIME.

CLASS 104.

47. **Colony of Assungui. Province of Paraná.** Specimens of SAPONACEOUS CLAYS, used especially for washing purposes.

48. **E. J. Gonzaga. Minas Novas; Province of Minas Geraes.** Specimens of CLAYS.

49. **J. Gonsalves. Rio Claro; Province of Rio de Janeiro.** CALCINED KAOLIN.

50. **G. Lourenço Correa. Jaboticabal; Province of S. Paulo.** Specimens of CLAYS.

51. **E. E. Wirmond. Lapa; Province of Paraná.** Specimens of Yellow ARGIL.

52. **C. S. da Mota. Province of Paraná.** TAGUA, a sort of rose-colored Argil.

53. **Commission General for the National Exhibitions. Rio de Janeiro.** CLAY of Jaboticabal.
   Specimens of violet-colored ARGIL, from S. Paulo.
   Specimens of SCHIST and ARGILS, from the Province of Alagoas.
   Specimens of red CLAY and red ARGIL, from Goyaz.

54. **Commission for the Province of Paraná. S. José dos Pinhaes; Province of Paraná.** HEMATITES, or BLOOD-STONES.

55. **T. G. C. Gomes. Antonina· Province of Paraná.** Specimens of ARGIL.

56. **D. J. Figueredo. Caçapava; Rio Grande do Sul.** White ARGIL and PLASTICS.

57. **Dr. F. T. S. Magalhaes. Camargos; Province of Minas Geraes.** Specimens of white TABATINGA, a sort of white ARGIL.
   Samples of colored CLAYS.

58. **J. F. d'Andrade. Jambeiro; Province of Minas Geraes.** Specimens of CLAYS of different colors.

59. **Commission for the District of Formiga. Formiga; Province of Minas Geraes.** Specimens of white and yellow ARGILS.

60. **A. Travanca. Porto de Cima; Province of Paraná.** White and yellow ARGIL, called commonly TABATINGA ARGIL.

61. **A. Schimmelpfing. Province of Paraná.** Specimens of KAOLIN

CLASS 106.

62. **Commission General for National Exhibitions. Rio de Janeiro.** Specimens of MINERALS, showing the gold and diamond formations, found in the Province of Goyaz.

Specimens of DIAMONDS-CONGLOMERATES, collected in the Province of "Minas Geraes."

DIAMONDS, found on the banks of "River Tibagy," in the Province of Paraná. (Diamonds are very abundant on the banks of this river, which course is distant 600 kilometers from the capital of the Province.)

63. **Dr. Agostinbo E. de Leão. Palmas; Province of Paraná.** DIAMONDS, found at "Palmas."

Specimens of yellowish ROCK-CRYSTALS, found at "Assungy." Specimens of AGATES, collected on the banks of "River-Tibagy," and at "Assungy."

64. **Dr. José C. da Silva-Muricy; Province of Paraná.** Specimens of QUARTZ, from Coritiba and Palmas.

Specimens of AGATES, found at "Guarapava."

Specimens of GRIND-STONE, from Coritiba.

65. **M. de Sã Ribas. Province of Paraná.** Specimens of ALUM, from Coritiba and Ponta Grossa. The Alum is very abundant in both places, but chiefly at "Ponta Grossa."

66. **Domingos F. Ferreira. Gavea; City of Rio de Janeiro.** Three DIAMONDS, weighing 23 carats, and of the value of fifteen thousand dollars.

One CUT-DIAMOND, value eight thousand dollars.

67. **L. Machado da Silva. Paranaguá; Province of Paraná.** Specimens of QUARTZ-PRISMS, from Paranaguá.

68. **Theodóro Heyd. Province of Paraná.** Specimens of GRIND-STONES, found on the banks of "Rio Negro," Province of Paraná. The Exhibitor claims the peculiar chemical composition of these stones, which contains the best *Clay* and *Schist.*

69. **P. Lustósa de Siqueira. Province of Paraná.** AGATES, from "Guarapava."

70. **National Muséum. Rio de Janeiro.** Specimens of GEMS, from different localities.

71. **Director General of the Colony of Mucury. Province of Minas Geraes.** Collection of PRECIOUS STONES, found in the Province.

72. **P. de Siqueira Cortez. Guarapava; Province of Paraná.** Specimens of violaceous QUARTZ, viz. : Amethyst

73. **Coritiba Muséum. Province of Paraná.** Specimens of violaceous QUARTZ.

74. **D. J. Santós Asevédo. Province of Goyaz.** DIAMONDS, found on the banks of "Rio Claro."

Specimens of MINERALS, showing the Gold and Diamond formations.

CLASS 107.

75. **D. Ferreira Maciel. Province of Paraná.** SULPHUREOUS WATER. Guarapava.

76. **Commission for the Province of Paraná.** ALKALINE WATERS from "Guarapava."

METALLURGICAL PRODUCTS.

CLASS 110.

77. **Commission General for the National Exhibitions. Rio de Janeiro.** Specimens of GOLD from "Goyaz."

78. **Commission for the Province of Paraná.** Specimens of VEINS OF GOLD, found in Felspathic Rocks.

79. **F. A. M. Tourinho. Province of Paraná.** Specimens of MAGNETIC GOLD, from "Rio Novo."

80. **J. Ewbank da Camara. Rio de Janeiro.** Specimens of AURIFEROUS STONES, from the Province of Rio de Janeiro.

81. **F. M. Leone and P. L. Lemos.** Province of Minas Geraes. AURIFEROUS MINERALS.

82. **F. T. Vieyra da Camara.** Province of Paraná. Specimens of GOLD DUST, found in Votuberaba.

83. **F. P. de A. Portugal.** Province of Paraná. Specimens of GOLD DUST found in Campo Largo.

CLASS III.

84. **Commission General for the National Exhibitions.** Rio de Jeneiro. Specimens of IRON MINERALS, from the Province of S. Paulo.

85. **Commission General for the Province of Pernambuco.** Specimens of NATIVE IRON, from Pernambuco.

86. **National Musuem.** Rio de Janeiro. Specimens of IRON AND COPPER, from different localities.

87. **The Presidency of the Province of Sancta Catharina.** Specimens of IRON AND NICKEL, found on the banks of S. Francisco River.

88. **B. A. da Cruz.** Province of Paraná. Specimens of MAGNETIC IRON.

89. **Ernesto Lellian.** Province of Paraná. Specimens of MAGNETIC IRON.

90. **S. Joao de Ypanema. Iron Works.** Province of S. Paulo. Specimens of BAR IRON.

91. **M. A. Machado da Silva.** Castro, Province of Paraná. Specimens of OLIGISTIC IRON.

92. **A. C. de Oliveira.** Fernandes; Coritiba, Province of Paraná. Specimens of OLIGISTIC IRON.

93. **Nemes Barboda.** Coritiba, Province of Paraná. Specimens of OLIGISTIC IRON.

94. **J. A. Vieyra de Aranjo.** Paranápanema, Province of Paraná. Specimens of OLIGISTIC IRON.

95. **Dr. Agostinbo E. de Ledo.** Antonina, Province of Paraná. Specimens of OLIGISTIC IRON.

96. **J. Francisco Supplicy.** Province of Paraná. MARCIAL PYRITES AND SULPHURATE OF IRON, found on the banks of the river Iguassu.

CLASS 113.

97. **Commission General for the National Exhibitions.** Rio de Janerio. Specimens of MERCURY from Palmeira, Province of Paraná.

98. **F. J. de Almeida Lopez.** Province of Paraná. SALTPETRE, found at Jaguariahiva.

99. **D. J. C. da Silva Muricy.** Compo-Largo, Province of Paraná. SULPHUR extracted from Quartz.

100. **F. Gasse.** Rio de Janeiro. LEAD FOILS, found at Rio de Janeiro (City.)

101. **D. Agostinbo S. E. Leão.** Province of Paraná. SULPHURATE OF LEAD, from the Environs of Coritiba. This Sulphurate contains a sort of Granular Galena, indicating the presence of silver.

MINE ENGINEERING.—MODELS, MAPS AND SECTIONS.

CLASS 120.

102. **Geological Commission.** Rio de Janeiro. Collection of GEOLOGICAL PHOTOGRAPHS of Brasil.

103. **Professor H. Gorceix.** Rio de Janeiro. GEOLOGICAL MAP of the Chapadão: Province of Minas Geraes.

DEPARTMENT II.
MANUFACTURES.

CHEMICAL

CLASS 200.

104. **L. B. Lendenberg.** Cape Frio; Rio de Janeiro. SALT.

105. **A. G. d'Araujo Penna.** Rio de Janeiro (City). HOMŒPATHIC VEGETABLE TINCTURES. OPODELDOC (Mikania Guaco.) This Opodeldoc is considered in Brazil as an excellent sudorific and antisyphlitic, and is used also as antidote for the bite of venemous snakes.

106. **Chemical Laboratory.** Rio de Janeiro. CHEMICAL and PHARMACEUTICAL PRODUCTS.

107. **Ferreira Maia & Co.** Pernambuco (City). PARMACEUTICAL PREPARATIONS.

108. **F. Aprigio da Yeiga.** Maceió; Province of Alagóas. PHARMACEUTICAL PRODUCTS. (Agricultural Hall.)

109. **F. J. Lepage.** Province of Minas Geraes. PHARMACEUTICAL PRODUCTS. (Agricultural Hall.)

110. **D. F. Z. Perdigão.** S. Luiy do Maranhão. PHARMACEUTICAL PRODUCTS.

111. **Commission for the Province of Maranhão.** PHARMACEUTICAL PREPARATIONS.

112. **Commission for the Province of S. Paulo.** MEDICAL PREPARATIONS.

CHEMICALS. 25

113. **E. Yiotti.** **Province of Paraná.** PHARMACEUTICAL PREPARATIONS.

114. **Duarte Dias.** **Rio de Janeiro.** DRUGS. (Agricultural Hall.)

115. **Commission for the Province of Ceará.** MEDICINAL OILS. (Agricultural Hall.)

116. **Commission for the Province of Pará.** MEDICINAL OILS.

117. **Leão Aloes.** **Parto Alegre, Province of S. Pedro do Sul.** PHARMACEUTICAL PREPARATIONS. (Agricultural Hall.)

118. **C. Falcon Dias.** **Maceió, Province of Alagoãs.** PHARMACEUTICAL PREPARATIONS. (Agricultural Hall.)

119. **Braga Juniar.** **Maceió, Province of Alagoãs.** PHARMACEUTICAL PREPARATIONS. (Agricultural Hall.)

120. **Military Hospital of Rio de Janeiro.** PHARMACEUTICAL PREPARATIONS, Ariquial, from Brazil. (Agricultural Hall.)

CLASS 201.

121. **Cardoso & Gonsalves** **Rio de Janeiro (City).** Samples of SOAP.

122. **Pereira Alves & Co.** **Province of Paraná.** Samples of SOAPS and CANDLES.

123. **Commission for the Province of Pernambuco.** SAFETY MATCHES.

124. **A. J. A. Guimarães.** **Rio de Janeiro (City).** SOAPS and CANDLES.

125. **Oliveira & Irmão.** **Province of Ceará.** SOAPS.

126. **Ferreira de Carvalho Irmão.** **Rio de Janeiro (City).** SOAPS and CANDLES.

127. **Company Luz Stearica.** **Rio de Janeiro (City).** SOAPS and CANDLES. A large amount of these products are consumed in the interior of Brazil, and also exported to foreign countries.

128. **Duarte Dias.** **Rio de Janeiro.** OILS.

129. **Commission for the Province of Paraná.** SOAPS AND CANDLES.

130. **J. Safarana.** **Paraná.** WAX CANDLES.

131. **Stechel.** **Province of Paraná.** OILS.

CLASS 202.

132. S. Samuel G. da Silva. Rio de Janeiro (City). COPYING and WRITING INKS.

133. Monteiro & Co. Rio de Janeiro (City.) WRITING INKS.

134. J. A. da Sa. Guimarães. Rio de Janeiro. PIGMENTS AND VARNISHES.

135. Commission for the Province of S. Paulo. WRITING INKS.

136. Yillela. S. Salvador da Bahia. WRITING INKS.

CLASS 203.

137. Daniel Henninger & Co. Rio de Janeiro (City.) SOAPS and TOILET SOAPS.

138. Lang & Co. Rio Grande; Province of S. Pedro do Sul. TOILET SOAPS.

139. Leão & Alves. Porto Alegre; Province of S. Pedro do Sul. PERFUMERY.

140. Otto Freire. Rio Grande do Sul. ESSENCES.

141. F. J. Lepage. Province of Minas Geraes ESSENCES AND POMADES.

142. Commission General for the National Exhibitions. Rio de Janeiro. FLAVORING EXTRACTS, ESSENCES AND PERFUMERY, from several Manufacturers.

143. J. Lang. Province of S. Pedro do Sul. TOILET SOAPS.

CERAMICS, POTTERY, PORCELAIN, &c.

CLASS 206.

144. F. A. M. Esberard. Rio de Janeiro (City). Terra Cotta Works. VASES, imitating the Etruscan style. OBJECTS OF POTTERY.

NOTE.—All these works are worthy of attention for their elegance and perfection.

145. **Colony of D. Francisca. Province of Sancta Catharina.** BRICKS AND TUBES OF CLAY.

146. **Commission General for the National Exhibitions. Rio de Janeiro.** Samples of BRICKS from the Province of S. Pedro do Sul.

147. **D. A. E. de Leão. Province of Paraná.** 1 BRICK OF GRES from "Campos Geraes." The district of Campos Geraes abounds in that kind of *gres* on a surface of 192 kilometers.

148. **Commission for the Province of S. Pedro do Sul.** STONE-BRICKS.

149. **Commission for the Province of Paraná.** TILES AND BRICKS.

CLASS 207.

150. **Amaro D. Grillo. Rio de Janeiro (City).** CLAY GOODS, POTS, CUPS AND VASES.

151. **J. J. S. Patury. Maceió; Province of Alagoas.** CLAY POTS, AND WATER-POTS.

CLASS 208.

152. **J. S. Correa. Assungy; Province of Paraná.** SLATE TILES for Pavements and Roofing.

153. **Dr. J. C. da Silva Muricy. Province of Paraná.** ENAMELED SLATE-TILES for Paving and Roofing. This sort of Slate comes in very great abundance from Campo Magro, Province of Paraná.

FURNITURE AND OBJECTS OF GENERAL USE IN CONSTRUCTION AND IN DWELLINGS.

CLASS 217.

154. **Commission General for the National Exhibitions.** A complete SET OF FURNITURE FOR PARLOR, after the Brasilian style. (That furniture which is exhibited in the Brasilian Pavillon, is made

of *Jacaranda* and *Rose woods*, and contains :—Two Shelves, one Sofa, four Arm-chairs, and twelve Chairs, all cane-bottomed. Chairs and Sofas made of different sorts of woods.

155. **Commission for the Province of Paraná.** DIFFERENT PIECES OF FURNITURE,

156. **Army Arsenal of Porto Alegre. Province of S. Pedro do Sul.** SECRETARY of Cedar-wood.

157. **House of Correction of Bahia S. Salvador da Bahia.** FURNITURE SUIT, made by the inmates.

158. **House of Correction of Rio de Janeiro. Rio de Janeiro. (City)** SECRETARY, inlaid with different sorts of woods. CABINET SUIT, made of *satin wood*, and containing, SOFA and six CHAIRS, all cane-seated.

159. **D. Clara Kern & Tela Lang. Province of Paraná.** RECLINING CHAIRS.

160. **Baron de "Itabapoana." Campos; Province of Rio de Janeiro.** RECLINING CHAIR.

161. **R. J. Gerth. Rio de Janeiro (City)** CABINET SUIT, and other objects, made of willow (vime).

162. **Edward Plauder. Colony of D. Francisca; Province of Sancta Catharina.** Objects made of Willow.

163. **Commission for the Province of Sancta Catharina.** WILLOW OBJECTS, made at the Colony of D. Francisca.

164. **Kappel & Irmão, Steam wood-work Factory. Province of S. Pedro do Sul.** COLLECTION OF WOOD-WORKS.

165. **J. C da Cósta Aguiar. Rio de Janeiro. (City).** BOOK STAND.

166. **J. F. Supplicy. Province of Paraná.** ETAGERE of Rose Wood. ETAGERE of "Embuia" and Sassafráz. WORK BOX for Lady. STOOLS, cane-seated.

167. **Zacharias Loesch. Province of Minas Geraes.** Small WORK-BOX, inlaid with different woods.

168. **F. J. Moreira & Co. Rio de Janeiro (City).** CHAIRS OF GENIPAPO, (a sort of Brazillian wood.)

NOTE.—The exhibitor disposes of a fine establishment, provided with steam machines and with a personal of 110 to 120 workmen. The wood employed in the works came exclusively from Brazil.

169. **D. J. Alipio. S. Salvador da Bahia.** WRITING DESK, made of Sole leather.

170. **A. A. Rodriguez. S. Salvador da Bahia.** WOODEN WRITING DESK.

171. **J. Neves d'Andrade. Province of Alagoãs.** BASKETS made of a sort of reed, called Maracajá in Brazil.

172. **Commission for the Province of S. Paulo.** SUIT OF FURNITURE, made of straw.

173. **Keppler & Irmão. Province of S. Pedro de Sul.** WOODEN CHAIRS

NOTE.—The Kappel & Irmão manufactury is entirely provided with steam machines, and furnishes now all the chairs used in the Province. That manufactory utilizes exclusively the national woods.

174. **Jonas Borddal. Province of Paraná.** TABLES, SHELVES, AND LADIES' WORK BOXES.

175. **Commission for the Province of Sancta Catharina.** VARIOUS PIECES OF FURNITURE.

176. **Polybio da Rocha. S. Salvador da Bahia.** MULTIFORM PIECE OF FURNITURE.

NOTE.—That piece can be transformed into ten other different pieces, and with the most comfortable proportions.

CLASS 218.

177. **Commission General for the National Exhibitions.** TORTOISE SHELL BOXES, made in the Province of Rio Grande do Nórte. STRAW ARTICLES, made in the Province of S. Paulo.

178. **Commission for the Province of Rio Grande do Nórte.** SMALL WOODEN CASES FOR JEWELRY. TORTOISE SHELL BOXES.

179. **Commission for the Province of Maranhão.** BATHING CUPS OF GOURD, varnished and colored.

Furniture and Objects in General Use, Etc.

180. **F. J. X. da Silva. Province of Paraná.** CHALICES AND CUPS made of Sassafraz and other woods.

181. **George Sabut. Rio de Janeiro (City).** Collection of ARTISTIC OBJECTS, made from Pine Tree Knots.

182. **Keppler & Irmãos. Porto Alegre; Province of S. Pedro do Sul.** CHAIRS, MOSAIC BOXES, MOULDINGS, made of Pine Wood.

183. **A. J. Gama Malcher. Cidade de Belem, Province of Pará.** STRAW SATCHELS AND SIEVES.

184. **House of Correction of Rio de Janeiro. Rio de Janeiro (City).** THREE BASKETS, BARREL, and STANDS for Manioc Farina.

185. **G. C. de Mello. Pernambuco (City).** WOODEN URN.

186. **J. J. d'Almeida. Rio de Janeiro.** GLASS CUPS, cut in Brazil.

CLASS 219.

187. **Commission for the Province of Rio Grande do Norte.** COCCO NUT SHELLS, Carved.

188. **Commission for the Province of S. Pedro do Sul.** MARBLE CROSS

189. **Martinelli & Irmão. Province of S. Paulo.** MARBLE APPURTENANCES FOR WASH-STAND.

190. **Adriano Pittanti & Co. Province of S. Pedro do Sul.** WASH-STAND OF SCULPTURED MARBLE.

191. **Léon Pommerais. Rio de Janeiro.** IMITATION OF MARBLES.

CLASS 224.

192. **J. Baumgarten. Cidade do Desterro; Province of Sancta Catharina.** ONE BOX with LOOKING-GLASS, for examining eggs.

YARNS AND WOVEN GOODS OF VEGETABLE AND MINERAL MATERIALS.

CLASS 228.

193. **A. Person.** Rio de Janeiro. WIRE-CLOTHS.

194. **F. Baidet.** Rio de Janeiro. WIRE CLOTHS AND WORKS.

CLASS 229.

195. **Commission General for the National Exhibitions. Rio de Janeiro.**
HAMMOCKS trimmed with feathers, made in the Province of Pará.
HAMMOCKS of cotton and cord, trimmed with feathers, made in the Province of Amazonas.
HAMMOCKS of cotton and cord, made in the Province of Ceará.
HAMMOCKS of Tucum, made in the Province of Ceará.

196. **Commission for the Province of Amazonas.** BROOMS AND CORDAGES OF RATTAN. (Agricultural Hall.)

CLASS 230.

197. **Commission General for the National Exhibitions. Rio de Janeiro.**
COTTON-GOODS AND GIRDLES, manufactured in Sobral, Province of Ceará.
COTTON-QUILTS, manufactured in the Province of Rio Grande do Nórte.
COTTON-GOODS, manufactured in the Province of Sergipe.

198. **Arouca & Co. Santo Antonio Cotton-Mills, Rio de Janeiro.** COTTON-GOODS.

199. **Rebello & Co. S. Pedro d'Alcantara Cotton-Mills. Province of Rio de Janeiro.** COTTON-GOODS.

VEGETABLE AND MINERAL MATERIALS.

200. Brazil Industrial Cotton Mills Co. (Fabrica de Tecidos—Brazil Industrial). Macacos; Province of Rio de Janeiro. COTTON-GOODS AND CANVAS of different qualities.

NOTE.—The establishment is one of the largest and most important which exists in Brazil; there are employed 400 looms, 60 carding-machines, and 20,000 spindles, and the production amounts at 8,000 metres of cotton-goods a day. The workmen are in number of 230, viz.: 125 men, 44 young men, 32 women, and 28 girls.

201. Colony Blumenau. Province of Sancta Catharina. COTTON-GOODS AND QUILTS.

202. Mascarenhas & Irmãos. Cedro Cotton-Mills; Province of Minas Geraes. COTTON-GOODS.

NOTE.—This establishment occupies a surface of 600 square metres, and employs the most modern machines. The number of workmen amounts to 53, and the average production is of 1,200 metres a day.

203. Diogo A. de Barros. Itú; Province of S. Paulo. COTTON-GOODS.

204. Anhaia & Angelo. Itú; Province of S. Paulo. COTTON-GOODS.

205. União Mercantil Co. Maceió, Province of Alagôas. COTTON-GOODS, from Fernão Yelho Cotton-Mills.

NOTE.—This establishment produces two kinds of woven goods.

206. Collegio da Immaculada Conceição; Province of Ceará. EMBROIDERED COTTON HAMMOCKS.

207. Yicary C. P. Sa. Curvello. Province of Alagôas. COTTON HAMMOCKS.

208. Commission for the Province of Paraná. TWISTED YARNS.

209. Petropolitana Co. Petropolis, Province of Rio de Janeiro. COTTON GOODS.

NOTE.—This establishment employs 100 workmen, 3500 spindles, 103 looms, and produces per day 6,000 metres of cotton goods.

CLASS 231.

210. Commission General for the National Exhibitions. Rio de Janeiro. DYED COTTON-GOODS, from the Province of Goyáz.

YARNS AND WOVEN GOODS, ETC.   33

211. **Barthelemy Chaná. Province of S. Pedro do Sul.** DYED GOODS.

212. **F. Reyner. Rio de Janeiro.** DYED GOODS.

CLASS 232.

213. **Commission General for the National Exhibitions. Rio de Janeiro.** COTTON TOWELS, made by hand, in the Province of S. Paulo.

214. **F. J. A. Lopez. Province of Paraná.** TOWELS, PANTALOONS and other articles of Cotton-wearing.

215. **Rosalina Z. Paes Leme. Province of Sancta Catharina.** Collection of COTTON FABRICS.

CLASS 233.

216. **Felippe Keller. S. João do Monte Negro Factory. Province of S. Pedro do Sul.** LINEN GOODS.

217. **Colony of St. Maria da Soledade; Province of S. Pedro do Sul.** LINEN GOODS.

218. **Instituto Fluminense d'Agricultura.** (Agriculture Fluminensis Institute). **Rio de Janeiro.** CIGAR CASES, HATS and other articles, made of the Bombanacea fibre. Five of the hats are the most worthy of attention.

219. **Colony Nóva Petropolis; Province of S. Pedro do Sul.** LINEN GOODS.

220. **Baron de Kalden. City of Cachoeira; Province of S. Pedro do Sul.** LINEN GOODS.

221. **Director of the Colony Sancta Maria da Soledade. Province of S. Pedro do Sul.** LINEN GOODS, middling and ordinary.

WOVEN AND FELT GOODS OF WOOL AND MIXTURES OF WOOL.

CLASS 235.

222. **F. J. Almeida Lopez. Province of Paraná.** Piece of WOOLEN-CLOTH. QUILTS. CASIMERES.

223. **Dr. J. C. Coelbo de Moura. Province of Minas Geraes.** CASSIMERES.

224. **Rheingantz & Vater. National Manufactory of Woolen Goods, Province of S. Pedro do Sul.** COLLECTION OF WOOLEN-GOODS.

    NOTE.—That manufactory has been established in 1874, in the city of Rio Grande, and covers an area of 1,500 square metres. The number of workmen averages 100 to 120, and the production attains 400 kilos of cloth a day, which corresponds to the average consumption of 300,000 kilogrammes of wool a year. The wool employed in the factory is exclusively taken from the sheep raised in the Province of S. Pedro do Sul.

CLASS 240.

225. **M. A. Machado. Province of Paraná.** Articles made of HORSES' HAIR.

SILK AND SILK FABRICS.

CLASS 243.

226. **Fernando Reyhner. Rio de Janeiro.** SILK-GOODS, CASSIMERES. Goods very much appreciated for their perfection and cheapness.

CLOTHING, JEWELRY AND ORNAMENTS.

CLASS 250.

227. **Ad. Dol & Co. Rio de Janeiro.** LINEN UNDERWEAR, for men and women.

228. **J. J. Roballo, Province of Paraná.** COAT of Fine Cloth.

229. **Frei L. da Grava. Ilhéos. Province of Espirito Sancto.** KNITTED SHIRT.

230. **Amaral & Co. Province of Para.** Complete SUIT, for gent.

231. **Fayett & Battcher. Province of S. Pedro do Sul.** PANTALOON, with one single seam.

CLASS 251. (ROOM C.)

232. **Commission General for the National Exhibitions. Rio de Janeiro.** Collection of WOODEN SHOES, from the Province of Paraná. (SHOES of Cordovan Leather, from the Province of Rio Grande do Nórte.)
HATS of Woven Cipó (a sort of reed,) from the Province of Rio Grande do Nórte.

233. **Chastel & Co. Rio de Janeiro.** HATS, of different qualities and sorts. Considered as one of the best qualities of Hats manufactured in Rio de Janeiro.

234. **J. Alvaro, d'Armada. Rio de Janeiro.** HATS, CAPS and BONNETS. (One of the largest and most important manufactory of Hats in Rio de Janeiro.

235. **Bierrenback & Irmãos. Campinas, Province of S. Paulo.** HATS and CAPS.

236. **Fernandes Braga & Co. Rio de Janeiro.** HATS, CAPS, and BONNETS. (All Hats of good quality, very light and cheap.)

Clothing, Jewelry and Ornaments.

237. J. Bithencourt, Rio de Janeiro. Lasts, for Shoes.

238. Viguier, Rio de Janeiro. Boots and Shoes.

239. J. B. Carvalho, da Silva, Rio de Janeiro. Hats, Baskets and other articles, made of *cipo-imbe*, (a sort of reed.)

240. J. E. P. Camará. Baturitè, Province of Ceara. Hats made from a peculiar sort of hay called in Brazil (Hen's foot hay.)

Note.—The Pé de Gallinha (Hen's foot hay) is a sort of *Graminæ*, which abounds near Rio de Janeiro, and almost in all Brazil; it belongs to the genus Dactylothenium.

241. City Council of Cameta. Province of Parā. Hats made of a sort of straw called Timboi, (*Bot. Carludovicea palmata.*)

242. P. C. dos Sāntos. Province of Alagoās. Shoes and Riding Boots.

243. H. Bossel. Province of S. Paulo. Felt Hats.

244. House of Correction of Rio de Janeiro. Rio de Janeiro. Boots and Shoes.

245. F. Fischer. Rio de Janeiro. Hats and Caps.

246. Figueredo & Co. Rio de Janeiro. Samples of Boots and Shoes furnished to the Brazilian Navy and Army.

247. C. F. Cathiard. Rio de Janeiro. Shoes and Boots. (All work made by machine.)

248. Berthon. Rio de Janeiro. Ladies' Shoes.

249. Commissioner for the District of Paulo Affonso. Province of Alagóas. Leather Hats from the interior of the country.

250. H. J. dā Silva. Province of Alagóas. Shoes of white canvas.

251. F. P. Requião. Rio de Janeiro. Hats for Gents and Boys of black-beaver and silk lined, grey-beaver and sheep-skin. These hats are remarkable for their lightness and cheapness, and show the perfection attained in this branch of industry.

252. F. Ficher. Province of S. Paulo. Silk Hat.

253. **M. M. Rodriguez Gomes. Province of Bahia.** BOOTS and SHOES for gents and ladies.
254. **Sertorio & Pinho. Rio de Janeiro.** KID GLOVES.
255. **H. Viguier. Rio de Janeiro.** SHOES provided with springs.
256. **J. C. de Moraes. S. Luiz, Province of Maranhão.** SILK HATS.

CLASS 252.

257. **M. J. Valentim. Rio de Janeiro.** ARTICLES OF JEWELRY.
258. **Victor Resse, Jr., & Irmãos. Rio de Janeiro.** Collection of BRAZILIAN DECORATIONS.

CLASS 253.

259. **Commission General for the National Exhibitions. Rio de Janeiro.** Collection of WALKING CANES from the Province of S. Paulo.
1 worn WALKING CANE and a collection of WHIP HANDLES.
1 WALKING CANE of Muirapinima. (Tortoise Shell Wood.)
260. **M'lle Natté. Rio de Janeiro.** Articles of FEATHERS, viz: fans, flowers, ornaments, coiffures, and insects mounted in gold. (This class of fancy work has no rival in the world.)
261. **Commission for Province of Amazonas. Rio Negro.** CROWN made of feathers.
262. **Dr. C. A. de Lima & J. M. de Calarans. Province of Rio Minas Geraes.** WAX, RIBBON AND FEATHER FLOWERS.
263. **A. J. F. Braga. Rio de Janeiro.** Collection of FEATHER ARTICLES AND FEATHER FLOWERS.
264. **J. S. H. Cavalcanti. Province of S. Paulo.** UMBRELLA with a secret spring.
265. **Henke & Irmãos. Province of Sancto Catharina.** WALKING CANES of Arabic wood.
266. **D. Rosalina Paes Leme. Province of Catharina.** LEATHER WALKING CANES.

267. **J. P. da. Rocha. Province of Bahia.** Collection of BUTTONS, EARRINGS and 1 WATCH CHAIN, all made of a small sort of cocconut.

268. **L. Gomes Ferreira. Rio de Janiero.** Collection of WALKING CANES.

269. **A. A. Barros. Province of S. Paulo.** WALKING CANES made of the cocco tree wood.

270. **José Xavier Bastos. Mar de Hespanha, Province of Minas Geraes.** 1 WALKING CANE made of *Peroba,* and carved.

271. **J. F. da Costa. Rio de Janeiro.** PICTURES OF MOSSES AND INSECTS.

272. **H. F. dos Reis. Province of Paraná.** WALKING CANE, imitating a parasol.

CLASS 256.

273. **Klippel & Irmão. Rio Grande; Province of S. Pedro do Sul.** HIDES AND FURS.

274. **F. Freischlag. Rio Grande; Province of S. Pedro do Sul.** PATENT LEATHER (Polished hides).

275. **Costa Eymael & Co. Rio Grande; Province of S. Pedro do Sul.** TANNED HIDES.

276. **F. G. S. Lima. S. Paulo; Province of S. Paulo.** TANNED LEATHER, sole.

277. **Jacob Richlin. Desterro, Province of Sancta Catharina.** TANNED LEATHER, sole.

CLASS 257.

278. **Commission General for the National Exhibitions.** A complete suit of HERDSMAN, made of leather.

PAPER, BLANKS, AND STATIONERY.

CLASS 261.

279. **Leusinger & Filhos.** Rio de Janeiro. BLANK BOOKS. (These books are entirely ruled, printed, bound, and finished in that establishment.)

2 BOUND VOLUMES (specimens of binding.)

280. **J. Seckler.** S. Paulo, Province of S. Paulo. 3 BOUND VOLUMES (specimens of ruling and binding).

MEDICINE, SURGERY, PROTHESIS.

CLASS 274.

281. **J. F. da Silva Garrid.** Province of S. Pedro do Sul. DRUGGIST SCALE.

282. **Merino & Co.** Rio de Janeiro. 43 SURGICAL INSTRUMENTS. (Amidst these instruments there are two invented by Dr. Fragoso, viz.: 1 incision knife for okymasis, and 1 electrolytic probe, two forceps modified by the exhibitors, and one upper and lower surgical key of their own invention.)

CLASS 277.

283. **M. F. da Silva Costa Jor.** Rio de Janeiro. ARTIFICIAL TEETH.
284. **J. Bento de Faria.** Rio de Janeiro. ARTIFICIAL TEETH.
285. **Dr. J. Borges Diniz.** Rio de Janeiro. ARTIFICIAL TEETH.

HARDWARE, EDGE-TOOLS, CUTLERY, Etc.

CLASS 281.

286. **Commission General for the National Exhibitions. Rio de Janeiro.**
KNIVES, DAGGERS, AND OTHER IMPLEMENTS, made in the Province of Paranà.

FABRICS OF VEGETABLE, ANIMAL, OR MINERAL MATERIALS.

CLASS 286 AND 287.

287. **Commission General for the National Exhibitions. Rio de Janeiro.**
BROOMS, BRUSHES, AND CORDAGES, from the Province of Amazonas.

CORDAGE, made of cotton thread, in the Province of Ceará.

288. **A. R. d'Almeida. Pernambuco.** CORDAGES, made of *carrapixo* (Bot. *Triumffetta semitriloba.*)

CARRIAGES, VEHICLES, HARNESS, AND ACCESSORIES.

CLASS 296.

289. **Commission General for the National Exhibitions. Rio de Janeiro.**
LEATHER SUIT AND HARNESS, used by herdsmen in the Province of Ceará.

SADDLE made in the Province of Sancta Catharina.

290. **A. A. A. Guimarães. Rio de Janeiro.** LADY'S SADDLE.

CARRIAGES, VEHICLES, HARNESS AND ACCESSORIES.

291. S. Maylasky. Province of S. Paulo. SERIGOTIS, a sort of leather *"horse belly-band"* used in that Province.

292. F. Gomes dos Santos Lima. Province of S. Paulo. HORSE BELLY-BANDS AND SERIGOTIS.

293. Baron de Cahy. Province of S. Pedro do Sul. 1 PAIR OF LEATHER REINS AND BRIDLES.

294. João Cranz & Pinto. Rio de Janeiro. HARNESS AND HORSE COLLARS.

295. Nicoláu Schmitt & Co. S. Leopoldo, Province of S. Pedro do Sul. A COMPLETE SET OF HARNESS, enameled by machine.

> NOTE.—The exhibitor got a privilege to employ a machine of his own invention in the manufacture of harness, and by that machine he is able now to execute by plates all the work made before by hand. The work is remarkable for its perfection and elegance.

296. T. T. A. Guimaraes. Rio de Janeiro. SADDLES.

> NOTE.—The exhibitor disposes of a large manufacture for leather work; his products are the most worthy of attention for their perfection and finish, and show the development of that branch of industry in Brazil.

297. Aimé Coullant. Rio de Janeiro. HORSE-COLLARS.

> NOTE.—These leather works are remarkable for the perfection of the workmanship and by the peculiar elegance of the pattern.

298. House of Correction of S. Paulo. BRIDLES, REINS AND HARNESS.

299. A. L. d'Almeida. Province of S. Paulo. REINS of leather.

300. T. C. Moraes. Province of Goyaz. 1 SADDLE of embossed leather.

301. J. de A. Barros. Province of S. Paulo. LEATHER REINS.

302. Waldemar Bierrengaard. Rio de Janeiro. RIDING HARNESS.

303. A. E. de Leão. Province de Paraná. 1 WHIP WITH WOODEN HANDLE imitating woven leather.

304. Å. A. Barros & B. A. Gaveão. Province of S. Paulo. 1 WHIP WITH SILVER HANDLE. 1 WHIP WITH WOODEN HANDLE carved with a pen knife.

305. Frederico Freischlag. Province of S. Pedro do Sul. Set of HARNESS, polished and trimmed with silver.

DEPARTMENT III.

EDUCATION AND SCIENCE.

EDUCATIONAL SYSTEMS, METHODS AND LIBRARIES.

CLASS 300.

306. Municipal School Boards. Rio de Janeiro. TEXT BOOKS.
SPECIMENS OF WRITING.
SPECIMENS OF DRAWING.
SAMPLES OF NEEDLEWORK.

307. Santa Candida School for Girls. Rio de Janeiro. Specimens of PENMANSHIP, remarkable for their neatness and excellence.

CLASS 302.

308. Faculty of Medicine. Rio de Janeiro. A collection of TEXT BOOKS and THESES on Medical and Chirurgical subjects.
NOTE.—This collection is remarkable for the variety of the subjects discussed and the proficiency of the authors.

309. Naval School. Rio de Janeiro. Collection of EDUCATIONAL BOOKS. Specimens of DRAWINGS and MODELS, made by the cadets. MAPS, CHARTS, ETC.
NOTE.—All the above collection is most worthy of attention, regarding the improved methods and the excellence of the cadets' work, and considering also that all the books have been written by Brazilian professors.

310. **Commercial Institute.** **Rio de Janeiro.** Specimens of DRAWING, WRITING and BOOKEEPING.

311. **Academy of Fine Arts.** **Rio de Janeiro.** Specimens of different styles of DRAWINGS, and pupils' works.

312. **Public Instruction Board.** **Rio de Janeiro.** EDUCATIONAL BOOKS, used in the lower and higher schools of the Empire.

　Specimens of WRITINGS and of NEEDLE-WORK intended to show the methods.

> NOTE.—The methods used now in Brazil for public schools are remarkable for their simplicity. The progress observed in the educational department is illustrated by the number of the schools and by the merit of the text books exhibited.

313. **Arts et Métiers Lyceums.** **Rio de Janeiro.** Specimens of DRAWINGS and PUPILS' WORKS.

314. **Artistical Institute.** **Rio de Janeiro.** CHROMO-LITHOGRAPHIC ENGRAVINGS.

　PRINTED BOOKS.

　MAPS and CHARTS.

　BOOK-BINDING specimens.

315. **Military Archives.** **Rio de Janeiro.** A collection of MAPS and CHARTS, drawn and engraved in the establishment.

316. **Faculty of Medicine.** **S. Salvador da Bahia.** Collection of THESES on medical subjects.

CLASS 303.

317. **Institute for Deaf and Dumb.** **Rio de Janeiro.** EDUCATIONAL BOOKS.

　Specimens of DRAWING and DACTYLOLOGICAL PAINTING.

　Specimens of WRITING.

　SHOES made by the pupils.

318. **Imperial Institute for Blind Boys and Girls.** **Rio de Janeiro.** Several APPARATUS used in teaching.

BOOKS printed, bound, and written by the blind boys.
GEOMETRICAL FIGURES, engraved by the blind boys, and MUSICAL COMPOSITIONS.
Specimens of NEEDLEWORK, made by the girls.

CLASS 304.

319. **Home Department.** Rio de Janeiro. EDUCATIONAL REPORTS. Laws, regulations, statistics and catalogues.

CLASS 306.

320. **Dr. Nicoláu J. Moreira.** Rio de Janeiro. TREATISE ON COLONIZATION.

321. **Dr. Nicoláu J. Moreira.** Rio de Janeiro. O AUXILIADÔR DA INDUSTRIA NACIONAL. (The National Industry Auxiliary Review.) This Review, published for nearly 40 years, for the propagation of Agricultural Industry, and Manufactures, and of their Improvement, received a prize at Vienna International Exhibition in 1873.

322. **Commission General for the National Exhibitions.** Rio de Janeiro. Collection of BRAZILIAN NEWSPAPERS.

323. **Leuzinger & Sons.** Rio de Janeiro. Specimens of PRINTING.

324. **Dr. Pessanha da Silva.** Rio de Janeiro. ANNAES BRASILIENSIS DE MEDECINA (Brazilian Medical annals), published monthly by the Imperial Academy of Medicine, of Rio de Janeiro, for nearly 30 years.

325. **Coronel J. M. Gaveaõ & Paesde Barros.** S. Paulo. NEWSPAPERS.

326. **J. Villeneuve & Co.** Rio de Janeiro. THE JOURNAL OF COMMERCE, bound.

327. **Rõxo, Monteiro & Lemos.** Rio de Janeiro. DIREITO MERCANTIL.

328. **E. Germack Possolo.** Rio de Janeiro. PRINTED BOOKS.

329. **S. José Alves.** Rio de Janeiro. PRINTED BOOKS.

330. **J. G. d'Azevedo.** Rio de Janeiro. PRINTED BOOKS.

331. **National Printing Office.** Rio de Janeiro. Specimens of MOULDS, TYPES, and PRINTED BOOKS.

332. **Nicolàu A. Alves** Rio de Janeiro. PRINTED BOOKS.

333. **Edward & Henry Laemmert.** Rio de Janeiro. PRINTED and BOUND BOOKS.

NOTE.—This was the first printing office established in Rio de Janeiro (1827), and is remarkable for the excellence of its printing and binding.

INSTITUTIONS AND ORGANIZATIONS.

CLASS 312.

334. **Leuzinger & Filhos.** Rio de Janeiro. Collection of articles for Museums.

335. **J. Ferreira d'A. Brant.** Minas Geraes. Collection of Insects.

336. **Narcisó & Arthur Napoleão.** Rio de Janeiro. MUSIC PRINTING and ENGRAVING.

337. **Quintino dos Santos.** Rio de Janeiro. MUSICAL COMPOSITIONS.

338. **Francisco Manuel da Silva.** Rio de Janeiro. MUSICAL COMPOSITIONS.

339. **Gomes d'Araujo.** Rio de Janeiro. MUSICAL COMPOSITIONS.

340. **Emilio do Lago.** Rio de Janeiro. MUSICAL COMPOSITIONS.

341. **J. J. Goyano.** Rio de Janeiro. MUSICAL COMPOSITIONS.

342. **J. A. da Silva Callado.** Rio de Janeiro. MUSICAL COMPOSITIONS.

343. **José Amat.** Rio de Janeiro. MUSICAL COMPOSITIONS.

344. **Cardoso de Menezes.** Rio de Janeiro. MUSICAL COMPOSITIONS.

345. **A. Campos.** Rio de Janeiro. MUSICAL COMPOSITIONS.

346. **Edward Ribas.** Rio de Janeiro. MUSICAL COMPOSITIONS.

SCIENTIFIC AND PHILOSOPHICAL INSTRUMENTS AND METHODS.

CLASS 320.

347. **Army Arsenal of Rio Grande do Sul.** Porto Alegre. METAL MERIDIAN, or Sun-Dial.

348. **Capt. Luiz de Saldanha, Brazilian Navy, Rio de Janeiro.** NAUTICAL REPEATING COMPASS.

349. **Lieut. A. Pereira Pinheiro. (Brazilian Navy).** Rio de Janeiro. SANDAGRAPH OR AUTOMATIC deep sea-sounding apparatus, (invention of the Exhibitor.)

MUSICAL INSTRUMENTS AND ACOUSTIC APPARATUS.

CLASS 327.

350. **Dr. Lamenha Lins.** Sancta Candida, Province of Paraná. 1 LARGE GUITAR, and 2 small ones (Machetes).

351. **J. dos Santos Couceiro.** Rio de Janeiro. 1 VIOLIN AND ITS BOW, made entirely of Brazilian woods.

352. **Commission General for the National Exhibitions.** Rio de Jeneiro. 1 PIANO.

ENGINEERING, ARCHITECURE, CHARTS, MAPS, AND GRAPHIC REPRESENTATIONS.

CIVIL ENGINEERING.

CLASS 330.

353. **The Board of Directors of the "Pedro II Dock works Company." Rio de Janeiro.** DRAWINGS, showing the "Pedro II Docks works," at Rio de Janeiro, and samples of the woods employed in the works, submarine constructions, wharves and warehouses.

354. **Engineers André Rebouças & Borja Castro. Rio de Janerio.** PHOTOGRAPHS representing the Custom-house Dock-works.
    Plans containing the details of these works, sections of the walls and foundations.

355. **Public Works Office. Rio de Janeiro.** Project to improve the harbors of the coast of Brazil, by Sir John Hawkshaw.

356. **Engineer E. Liais. Rio de Janeiro.** SURVEYS and PROFILES of the rivers das "Velhas" and S. Francisco, accompanied by a minute report on the works required for improving their navigation.

357. **Hydrographic Department. Rio de Janeiro.** SURVEYS of the Amazonas river from its mouth to the boundary of Brazil with Peru, over an extension of 2,240 miles, by Commander Soares Pinto (Brazilian navy), and the Engineer Pereira Dias, under the direction of Captain Costa Azevedo (Brazilian navy.)

RAILWAY ENGINEERING.

CLASS 332.

358. **W. Speir. Province of S. Paulo.** DRAWINGS of the railroad from Santos to Jundiahy, S. Paulo.

359. **Dr. Ewbanck. Rio de Janeiro.** Description of the RAILWAYS of the Province of S. Paulo.

360. **Engineer Fox. Province of S. Paulo.** General PLAN and PROFILES of the railway from Santos to Jundiahy.
DRAWINGS of the viaduct over "Grota Funda," on the same railway.

361. **Public Works Office. Rio de Janeiro.** Various DRAWINGS, showing the bridges of the Pedro II. railway.

362. **Engineer Ferreira Penna. S. Pedro do Sul.** PLANS, ESTIMATES and REPORT on the projected railway from Porto Alegre to Uruguayana, Province of S. Pedro do Sul.

363. **Engineer Loyd. Rio de Janeiro.** PROJECT of a railway to the Province of Matto Grasso, with illustrations, plans, estimates and profiles.

364. **Engineer Bulhões. Rio de Janeiro.** PROJECT to lengthen the main railway line of the Province of Bahia, with illustrations, plans, and estimates.

365. **Engineer Silva Coutinho. Rio de Janeiro.** PROJECT to lengthen the main railway line of the Province of Pernambuco, with illustrations and plans

TOPOGRAPHICAL AND GEOLOGICAL MAPS AND SECTIONS.

CLASS 335.

366. **Commission General for the National Exhibitions. Rio de Janeiro.** Collection of MAPS OF THE PROVINCE OF S. PAULO.
    Elements for the organization of a PHYSICAL CHART OF BRAZIL, by the Councilor " Homen de Mello."
367. **Senator C. Mendes. Rio de Janeiro.** ATLAS of the Brazilian Empire.
368. **General de Beaurepaire Rohan. Rio de Janeiro.** General CHART of the Empire of Brazil.
369. **Public Works Office. Rio de Janeiro.** CHARTS and TOPOGRAPHICAL MAPS of the Provinces of S. Paulo, Sancta Catharina, Maranhão, Ceará, Goyaz, Paraná, Espirito Sancto, Minas Geraes, and Piauhy.
    CHARTS of the projected Provinces of S. Francisco, Entre Rios, Sapucahy and Araguaya.
    MAPS of the public lands of the Province of S. Paulo.
    TOPOGRAPHICAL MAP of the Colony Blumenau.
370. **Hydrographic Department. Rio de Janeiro.** CHARTS of the coast and harbors of Brazil.

PHYSICAL, SOCIAL AND MORAL CONDITION OF MAN.

MONEY, MINTS AND COINING.

CLASS 344.

371. **National Mint. Rio de Janeiro.** Collection of MEDALS marked in the Mint. Collection of BRAZILIAN COINS.
372. **J. F. Suplicy. Province of Paraná.** Collection of MEDALS obtained by Galvanoplastic process. 1 GALVANOPLASTIC PILE.

DEPARTMENT IV.

ART.

---o---

SCULPTURE.

---o---

CLASS 400.

373. **Academy of Fine Arts. Rio de Janeiro.** STATUE IN PLASTER. Recollection of the Tribe, by Bernardelli.

   STATUE IN PLASTER. The actor, Joao Caetano, acting as Oscar, by Chaves Pinheiro.

   STATUE IN PLASTER. The Indian Peeping, by Bernardelli.

374. **Almeida Reis. Rio de Janeiro.** STATUE IN PLASTER. The Crime, by the exhibitor.

375. **Almeida Reis. Rio de Janeiro.** STATUE IN PLASTER. The Bishop of Chrysopolis, by the exhibitor.

PAINTING.

CLASS 410.

376. **Academy of Fine Arts. Rio de Janeiro.** Painting in OIL ON CANVAS. The naval battle of "Riachuelo," (Paraguayan war) by Victor Meirelles.

   Painting in OIL ON CANVAS. The First Mass in Brazil, by Victor Meirelles.

   Painting in OIL ON CANVAS. "The Brazilian iron-clad fleet passing by Humaitá" (Paraguayan war), by Victor Meirelles.

377. **Academy of Fine Arts. Rio de Janeiro.** Painting in OIL ON CANVAS. "View of St. Peter's Cathedral in Rome."
Painting in OIL ON CANVAS. "Charity."
378. **Public-works office. Rio de Janeiro.** Painting in OIL ON CANVAS. Brazilian army crossing "PASSO da Patria (Paraná river) led by Marshall Ozorio during Paraguayan war, by Pedro Americo.
Painting in OIL ON CANVAS. Moonlight in the harbour of Montevideo (River Plate), by De-Martino.
379. **Senate Hall. Rio de Janeiro.** Painting in OIL ON CANVAS. Defence of the Island of Cabrita, by Brazilian army and navy (Paraguayan war), painted by Pedro Americo.
380. **H. Henschell. Rio de Janeiro.** PORTRAIT OF HIS MAJESTY THE EMPEROR OF BRAZIL, in oil on canvas, by the exhibitor.
381. **His Royal Highness, the Count d'Eu. Rio de Janeiro.** Painting in OIL ON CANVAS, representing a scene at sunset on a seashore.

WATER-COLOR PICTURES, AQUARELLES, MINIATURES.

CLASS 411.

382. **J. Insley Pachèco. Rio de Janeiro.** OIL AND WATER-COLOR PICTURES representing views of the interior of Brazil; aquarelles.
383. **Antonio da Rocha. Rio de Janeiro.** MINIATURE, copy of the Virgin of Guido Reni.
384. **Souza da Silveira. Rio de Janeiro.** TRANSPARENT MINIATURES.

ENGRAVING AND LITHOGRAPHY.

DRAWINGS WITH PEN, PENCIL OR CRAYONS.

CLASS 420.

385. **Marianno d'Almeida. Rio de Janeiro.** DRAWINGS with pen and ink.

386. Insley Pachéco. Rio de Janeiro. Two LANDSCAPES with Crayons.

387. João dos Passos Damasceno. Brazil. PORTRAITS OF HIS MAJESTY THE EMPEROR OF BRAZIL, drawn with pen and ink.

LITHOGRAPHS AND ZINCOGRAPHS.

CLASS 423.

388. Jayme Brutens. S. Paulo. LITHOGRAPHS.

389. H. Carlls. Pernambucco. LITHOGRAPH SPECIMENS.

390. N. N. Rio de Janeiro. LITHOGRAPHS.

391. Edward Rensburg. Rio de Janeiro. LITHOGRAPHICAL MAPS AND DRAWINGS, (Main Building.)

392. A. Sisson. Rio de Janeiro. LITHOGRAPHICAL WORKS.

PHOTOGRAPHIC HALL.

PHOTOGRAPHY.

PHOTOGRAPHS ON PAPER, METAL, GLASS, Etc.

CLASS 430.

393. **I. Insley Pachéco. Rio de Janeiro.** PHOTOGRAPHS; Portraits after the system of bichromotype (invention of the exhibitor.)

394. **P. S. de Souza da Silveira. Rio de Janeiro.** PHOTOGRAPHS.

395. **Leuzinger Sons. Rio de Janeiro.** PANORAMAS of Rio de Janeiro in Photo-Lithograph. (Annex of Art Gallery.)

396. **Thomas Sabino. Belém. Province of Pará.** PHOTOGRAPHS.

397. **N. N. Rio de Janeiro.** PHOTOGRAPHS.

398. **Luiz Terragno. Province of S. Pedro do Sul.** PHOTOGRAPHS.

399. **Fidanza. Belém. Province of Pará.** PHOTOGRAPHS.

DEPARTMENT V.

―o―

APPARATUS AND FIXTURES FOR HEATING AND COOKING.

―o―

CLASS 222.

400. **J. A. Antunes. Rio de Janeiro.** COFFEE POTS for cooking Coffee.

BATH ROOMS AND WATER CLOSETS.

401. **M. Alves Marques Jor. Rio de Janeiro.** MECHANICAL SHOWER-BATH made of Tin, presenting an architectural appearance. (Patent of the exhibitor.)

ARMY AND NAVY.

PYROTECHNICS.

CLASS 205.

402. **Pyrotechnical Laboratory of Campinho. Rio de Janeiro.** ROCKETS used in war as missiles.
 METALIC FUZES for shells of either light or heavy artillery.
403. **Military Archives. Rio de Janeiro.** PYROTECHNICAL MAPS.
404. **Dr. Fausto de Souza, Director of the Pyrotechnical Laboratory of Camphino. Rio de Janeiro.** METALIC FUZES for shells. APPARATUS FOR FIRING FUZES. (Invention of the exhibitor.)

MILITARY CLOTHING.

CLASS 250.

405. Army Arsenal. Rio de Janeiro. UNIFORMS AND EQUIPMENTS worn by the different Corps of the Brazilian Army.

FANCY LEATHER WORK, VALISES AND TRUNK.

CLASS 255.

406. Army Arsenal. Rio de Janeiro. A pair of VALISES, showing the pattern adopted for officer's service in campaign.

MILITARY AND NAVAL ARMAMENTS, ORDNANCE, FIRE-ARMS AND HUNTING APPARATUS.

MILITARY SMALL-ARMS, PISTOLS, MAGAZINE, GUNS, ETC.

CLASS 265.

407. Army Arsenal. Rio de Janeiro. 1 BREECH LOADING RIFLE AND SWORD BAYONET, entirely made after the model proposed by Major Moraes Ancora, of the Engineer corps, and adopted for the Brazilian army after the most successsul trials.

REVOLVER, invented and made by hand by the artizan of the Arsenal, Mr. Augusto Teixeira.

BREECH LOADING RIFLE, invention and work of the artizan of the Arsenal, Mr. T. Eustachio de Gusmao.

408. Arsenal of Bahia. DRUM of the pattern adopted for Brazilian Army and Navy.

409. Pyrotechnical Laboratory of Campinho. Rio de Janeiro. AMMUNITION for rifles and revolvers.

410. Dr. Fausto de Souza, Director of the Pyrotechnical Laboratory of Campinho. Rio de Janeiro. MACHINE TO MAKE METALLIC CARTRIDGES FOR RIFLES AND REVOLVERS. (This machine is an invention of the engineer, Otto Anderson.)

LIGHT ARTILLERY, COMPOUND GUNS, ETC.

CLASS 266.

411. Army Arsenal. Rio de Janeiro. THREE BRASS FIELD GUNS, rifled on French system; caliber,—12 pounder, 4 pounder (heavy), and 4 pounder for service on mountains.

WOODEN CARRIAGE, for 4 pounder Field gun, and accessories.

MODEL OF 12 POUNDER RIFLED FIELD-GUN, with carriage and limber, and accessories.

DRAWINGS, showing the pattern of carriages, caissons and limbers, adopted for Brazilian army.

SHOTS AND SHELLS FOR FIELD GUNS, of Krupp, Withworth and French systems.

HEAVY ORDNANCE AND ITS ACCESSORIES.

CLASS 267.

412. Army Arsenal. Rio de Janeiro. THREE BRASS MORTARS AND THEIR PLATFORMS; calibers,—0.27m., 0.22m. and 0.15m.

MODEL OF CASEMATE AND OF A 300 POUNDER WITHWORTH'S RIFLED GUN (muzzle loader), mounted on a carriage of Scott's system, all showing what is adopted for Brazil's sea-coast and harbour defence.

SHOTS AND SHELLS for heavy guns of Withworth's system.

413. Navy Arsenal. Rio de Janeiro. LEATHER BUCKETS for artillery service.

LEATHER CARTRIDGE-BOXES for heavy ordnance.

HARDWARE, EDGE TOOLS, CUTLERY AND METALIC PRODUCTS.

KNIVES, SWORDS, SPEARS, ETC.

CLASS 268.

414. Army Arsenal. Rio de Janeiro. SWORD FOR CAVALRY, showing the pattern adopted for Brazilian army.

FOUR SPEARS of the pattern adopted for the regiments of Lancers.

415. Arsenal of Porto Aiegre. Province of S. Pedro do Sul. PECULIAR WEAPONS used by the cavalry of the Brazilian army.

HAND TOOLS.

CLASS 280.

416. Arsenal of Bahia. HAND TOOLS AND INSTRUMENTS used by carpenters and joiners.

417. Siloino Trispode. Province of S. Pedro de Sul. HAND TOOLS.

418. Ypanema Iron Works. Province of S. Paulo. HAND TOOLS.

METAL HOLLOW WARE ORNAMENTAL CASTINGS.

CLASS 283.

419. Ypanema Iron Works. Province of S. Paulo. ONE CROSS, AND ONE IMPERIAL CROWN OF CAST IRON, samples of cast iron, bars.

NOTE.—This establishment employs a personal of 121 workmen, and disposes of a complete set of machines to obtain the iron of the ores and to work it. The production of ferro emguza amounts to 3,000 kil. a day. The establishment was obliged to use, until now, the vegetable coal, but at present the discovery of splendid mines of coal distant scarcely 37 kilometres, promises to supply it abundantly with a good sort of combustible.

420. **Bierrenback & Irmão. Cast Iron Works, Province of S. Paulo.** ONE CHAIR AND SEVERAL GRATES of CAST IRON; samples of ornamental iron-castings.

421. **Couto dos Santos. Rio de Janeiro.** IMPERIAL CROWN of cast-iron, BUST OF THE EMPEROR AND EMPRESS OF BRAZIL, made in cast-iron; samples of ornamental iron castings, remarkable for their elegance and beauty of finish.

422. **Hargreaves & Irmãos. Rio de Janeiro.** ORNAMENTAL IRON CASTINGS, one Imperial Crown the Escutcheon of His Royal Highness the Count d'Eu; the Escutcheon of His Highness the Duke of Saxe.

423. **Ponta d'Aréa Works Company. Rio de Janeiro.** IMPERIAL CROWN of cast-iron and guilt.

424. **Army Arsenal. Rio de Janeiro.** Different pieces aud ornaments of an iron stair case.

HARDWARE.

CLASS 284.

425. **Arsenal of Bahia.** LOCKS for naval and shipstores, locks for safes.
426. **Army Arsenal. Rio de Janeiro.** MODELS OF SAFES used by the Staff and Engineers Corps of the Brazilian army.
427. **Fabiano Slickel. Rio de Janeiro.** HORSE SHOES of different shapes.
428. **Hargreaves & Irmãos. Rio de Janeiro.** IRON BARS AND IRON STANDS.
429. **Ypanema Iron Works. Province of S. Paulo.** HOOKS, SPIKES, BOLTS, and IRON BARS.

FABRICS OF VEGETABLE, AND MINERAL MATERIALS.

ROPES, CORDAGE.

CLASS 287.

430. Navy Arsenal of Rio de Janeiro. Ropes, cords, and lines, for naval purposes.

CARRIAGES AND ACCESSORIES.

HARNESS AND SADDLERY.

CLASS 296.

431. Army Arsenal. Rio de Janeiro. PIG-SKIN SADDLE, REINS AND BRIDLES, trimmed with golden thread as used for the horse furniture of the officers of Brazilian army.

Complete set of HARNESS of the pattern adopted for Brazilian Cavalry and Horse Artillery.

ENGINEERING, ARCHITECTURE AND MAPS.

CIVIL ENGINEERING.

CLASS 330.

432. Navy Arsenal. Rio de Janeiro. MODELS OF 2 DRY-DOCKS cut into granite rock.

MACHINERY.

MACHINES AND TABLES FOR MARKING METAL, WOOD AND STONE.

PLANING, CUTTING, MOULDING, STAMPING MACHINES, ETC.

CLASS 510.

433. **The National Mint. Rio de Janeiro.** 1 STAMPING MACHINE.
One EDGING MACHINE.
HAND-TOOLS AND INSTRUMENTS.

MACHINES FOR THE MANUFACTURE OF SILK.

CLASS 520.

434. **Luiz de Rezende.   Sericiculture Establishment.   Rio de Janeiro.**
One MACHINE FOR REELING AND SKEINING SILK.
APPARATUS FOR COUNTING THE TWIST.
STEREOMETER AND SCALES.
Samples of SILK of the "Butter Fly," "Aurota Saturnia," reeled and twisted.
VIEWS, description and pictures of the establishment.
NOTE.—This Department is most worthy of public attention, and demonstrates the great advancement of the "*Sericiculture*" in Brazil.

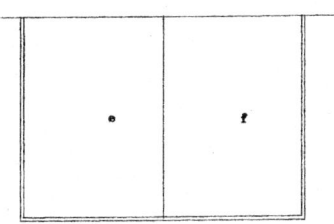

A. A.—Navy Department.
B. B.—Army   "
C. C.—Mint.
D.—Pump Department.
E.—Silk Machines.
F.—Ornamental Castings.

Machinery Hall.

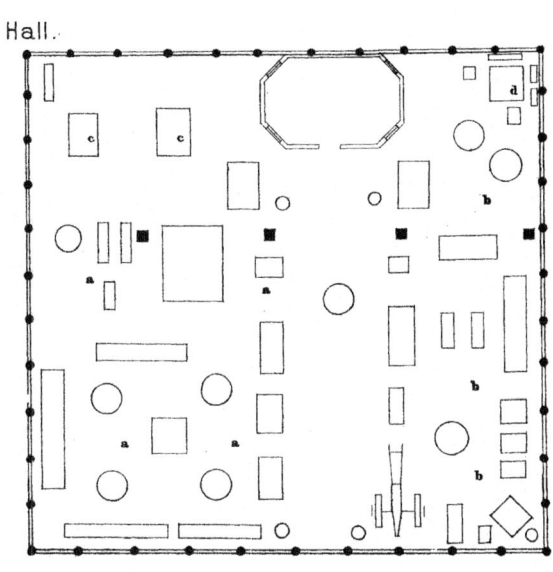

Machinery Hall.
Scale ⅙ Inch = one foot.

MOTORS AND APPARATUS FOR THE GENERATION AND TRANSMISSION OF POWER.

STEAM, AIR OR GAS ENGINES, ETC.

CLASS 550.

435. **Navy Arsenal. Rio de Janeiro.** DUPLEX STEAM ENGINE, 12 nominal horse power, to be used as motor at the Pyrotechnical Laboratory da Armação. (Rio de Janeiro.)
MODEL OF THE DUPLEX ENGINES built for the iron-clads of the Monitor class.
MODEL OF THE ENGINES built for " Mortar Ships."

436. **Navy Arsenal. Bahia.** MODEL OF a MARINE LOCOMOTIVE.

APPARATUS FOR THE TRANSMISSION OF POWER.

CLASS 552.

437. **Navy Arsenal. Rio de Janeiro.** PULLEYS, PULLEYS STAND-SHAFTS AND FLYING WHEELS.

SCREW-PROPELLERS, WHEELS, ETC.

CLASS 554.

438. **Army Arsenal. Rio de Janeiro.** IRON SCREW PROPELLER AND ITS COG-WHEEL.

HYDRAULIC AND PNEUMATIC APPARATUS, PUMPING, HOISTING AND LIFTING.

PUMPS AND APPARATUS FOR LIFTING AND COMPRESSING FLUIDS.

CLASS 560.

439. **T. Candido da Costa, Pump Maker.** Rio de Janeiro. Two DUPLEX LIFTING AND FORCE PUMPS, hand power.
One DUPLEX LIFTING AND FORCE PUMP, hand power.
Two single LIFTING AND FORCE PUMPS, either hand or steam-power.
Two single LIFTING AND FORCE PUMPS, hand power.
One HYDRAULIC RAM.

STOP-VALVES, COCKS, PIPES, ETC.

CLASS 566.

440. **T. Candido da Costa.** Rio de Janeiro. One NOZZLE FIRE PLUG.
441. **F. Candido das Neves.** Rio de Janeiro. COCKS of different systems.
442. **B. G. Russell.** Rio de Janeiro. LEAD PIPES AND HYDRAULIC SYPHONS.
COPPER VALVE BOX for shower bath.

MACHINES USED IN PREPARING AGRICULTURAL PRODUCTS.

FLOUR MILLS.

CLASS 580.

443. **Birrenback & Irmãos, Iron Works.** Province of S. Paulo. HAND MILL to grind manioc roots.

ÆRIAL, PNEUMATIC AND WATER TRANSPORTATION.

STEAM SHIPS, STEAMBOATS AND ALL VESSELS PROPELLED BY STEAM.

CLASS 595.

444. **Navy Arsenal. Rio de Janeiro.** MODELS OF ALL SHIPS built on the stocks of the Arsenal, including models of iron-clads, casemate and turret ships; wooden ships of all classes; steam-launches, and the models of the corvettes and launches designed by the Naval Constructor, Trajano Carvalho.

    Samples of the WOODS used in the Arsenal for ship building.

445. **Trajano A. Carvalho, Ship Constructor. Rio de Janeiro.** MODELS OF TWO CORVETTES AND ONE STEAM LAUNCH, built according to the novel formation of bottom of ships, invented by the exhibitor himself.

    NOTE.—The exhibitor claims the following advantages for his new lines:

    1st. As the ship moves ahead in an upright position, there are no forces created either on the sides or under the floor tending to raise the bow, and so that this most important element of resistance is avoided.

    2d. High speed with the most moderate proportions of length to breadth.

    3d. For a vessel of any proportion of length to breadth the requisite displacement may be obtained with a much finer entrance than usual, and without the less disadvantage in the form of the after body.

    4th. Superiority of displacement on the same dimensions.

STEAM CAPSTANS, FANS, ETC.

CLASS 597.

446. **Army Arsenal. Rio de Janeiro.** FAN OF CAST IRON, steam power.

DEPARTMENT VI.

AGRICULTURE.

---o---

ARBORICULTURE AND FOREST PRODUCTS.

---o---

CLASS 600.

447. **Commission General for the National Exhibition. Rio de Janeiro.**
Samples of WOODS from the Province of Bahia.
Samples of WOODS from the Province of Goyaz.
Samples of WOODS from the Province of "Rio Grande do Norte."
Samples of WOODS from the Province of S. Pedro do Sul.

448. **Commission for the Province of Paranà.** Samples of WOODS used in ship building, engineering works and in decorating.

449. **Pedro II. Dock Works Company. Rio de Janeiro.** Samples of WOODS used in the Dock Works for submarine construction of wharves and storehouses.

450. **Commission for the Province of "Bahia."** Samples of WOODS used in construction and for furniture.

451. **Commission for the Province of Pernambuco.** Samples of WOODS used for building and furniture.

452. **Commission for the Province of Sancta Catharina.** Samples of WOODS used in constructions and for furniture.

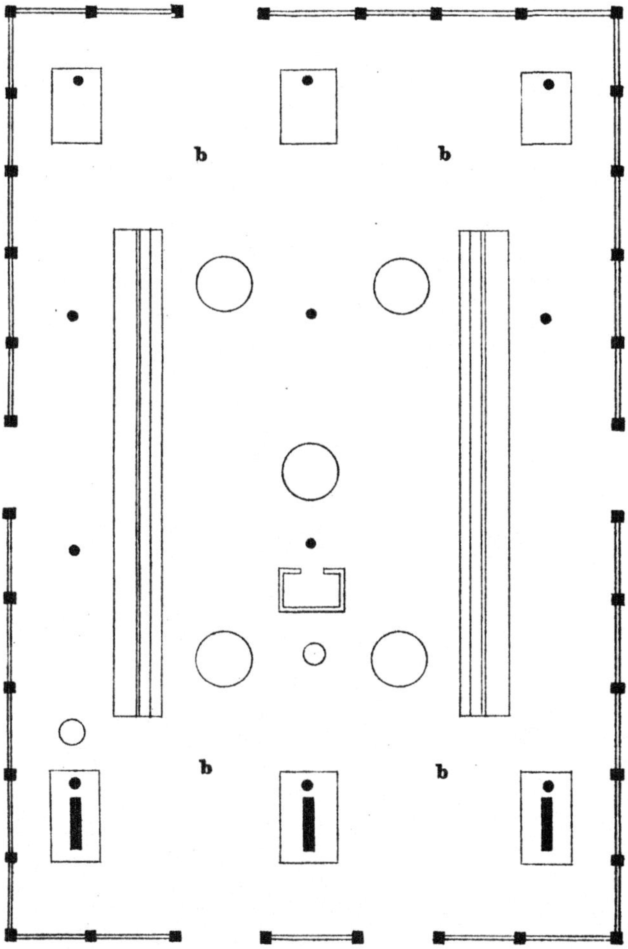

A. A.—Coffee and Cotton.
B. B.—Forest and Agricultural Products.

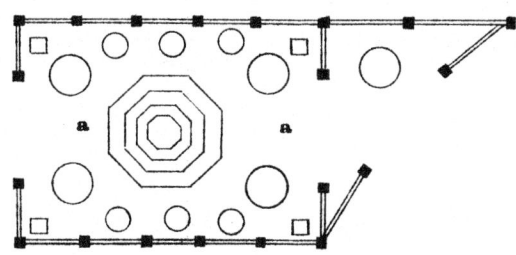

Agricultural Hall
Scale 1/16 Inch = one foot.

ABORICULTURE AND FOREST PRODUCTS.

453. **Commissioner of the Province of S. Paulo.** Samples of WOODS used in ship building and civil engineering works and for furniture.

454. **C. B. de S. Farie. Rio de Janeiro.** Samples of WOODS from S. João do Barra, Province of Rio de Janeiro.

455. **Baron de Villa Franca. Quissamã, Province of Rio de Janeiro.** Samples of WOOD.

456. **Baron de Juparanà and Nogeira da Gama. Valença, Province of Rio de Janeiro.** Samples of WOODS.

457. **Director of the Colony of Itajahy. Province of Sancta Catharina.** Samples of WOODS used in construction and for furniture.

458. **J. M. C. Cavalcanti. Province of Alagōas.** Samples of WOODS used in constructions, ship building, civil engineering works and for furniture.

459. **J. F. Barbósa. Province of Maranhaõ.** Samples of WOODS.

460. **Dr. Borja Castro. Rio de Janeiro.** Samples of WOODS used in the Custom House Dock Works.

461. **Commission for the Province of Rio de Janeiro. Niçtheroy.** Samples of WOODS.

462. **Dr. Muricy. Province of Paraná.** COAL obtained from pine tree (Araucaria Braziliensis).
Samples of WOODS.

463. **Dr. Hermelino de Leaõ. Province of Paraná.** COAL obtained from Pine tree knots (Araucaria Braziliensis).
Samples of WOODS.

464. **Araujo de Silva. Campos. Province of Rio de Janeiro.** Samples of WOODS.

465. **Domingos Silva. Province of Rio de Janeiro.** Samples of WOODS.

466. **Pimenta Bueno. Province of Pará.** Samples of Woods, from the valley of Amazonas.

467. **Commission for the Province of Goyaz.** PAPARUS, or paper tree; Samples of WOODS.

468. Commission for the Province of Amazonas. Samples of WOODS. ISCA DE URACOA, made by ants.

CLASS 601.

469. Azarias C. Gama. Province of Alagôas. CIPO PAO, a sort of vine used for making walking canes.

470. Dr. Muricy and Dr. Leão. Province of Paraná. Samples of PINE TREE KNOTS, used for making ornamental objects.

471. Couceiro. Rio de Janeiro. Samples of WOODS, for decorating, arranged in Mosaic.

472. Municipality of S. Francisco. Province of Sancta Catharina. Samples of some ORNAMENTAL WOODS, viz.. "Canella Amarella," (Bot. *Nectandra sp*). "Ebony," "Gissarana," and " Maiato."

473. Municipality of S. José. Province of Sancta Catharina. Samples of ORNAMENTAL WOODS.

CLASS 602.

474. Commission General for the National Exhibitions. Rio de Janeiro. FRAME made with samples of woods.

475. Commission for the Province of Amazonas. ANILEIRA (Indigo wood), (Bot. *Indigofera tinctoria*), which produces an excellent blue dye.

NOTE.—There are many different species of *Indigoferos* in the Valley of Amazonas and on the Platean of the Guianes, viz —*anil, tinctoria, argentea*, &c., all remarkable for the excellent dye, which can be extracted from their leaves.

CARAJUIE (Bot. *Bignonia chica*), producing an excellent red dye.

NOTE.—The *carajuie* is considered as the best American red dye; its leaves are also highly esteemed for their medicinal virtues.

476. J. F. Guimarães & Co. Province of Paraná. RAVE DE S. JONO, (a sort of shrub which produces a beautiful yellow dye for coloring.

477. **Rev. Daniel P. M. d'Oliveira. Province of Amazonas.** Samples of CUMATE (Bot. *Asclepiadacea ? Apocynaceas ?*). That sort of wood produces the best black ink.

478. **J. F. Andrade Branl. Province of Minas Geraes.** Samples of BARKS, used for coloring.

479. **Commission for the Province of Pernambuco.** Samples of GITÒ MIRIM. (Bot. *Guarea Trichilioides*), used for coloring.

480. **Commission for the District of Anadia. Province of Alagôas.** Samples of CORONA-CHRISTI, a sort of wood which produces good ink and resin.

481. **Commission for the Province of Ceará.** Samples of URUCU. (Bot. *Bixa-orellana;* Acafròa Curcumæ tinctoria.)

    NOTE.—The *Urucu* produces a dark yellow dye for coloring.

    TASSUANA (*Indigofera*), remarkable for its large width.

    NOTE.—The Tassuana produces a very fine blue dye.

CLASS 603.

MANGUE DE SAPATEIRO (Rhyso-sophora mangle).

   NOTE.—This wood produces a black dye ink, and is largely used for tanning leather.

482. **Dr. R. Rebello. Breves, Province of Pará.** BARK of Tauari (Courataritanari.)

    NOTE.—This bark is also used for making cigarettes.

483. **I. Tldelfonso J. G. d'Andrade. Province of Paraná.** BARK of Angico (Acacia Angico).

484. **Commission General for the National Exhibitions. Rio de Janeiro.** PAPER TREE (Læsiandra-papyrus), from the Province of Goyaz.

    NOTE.—This sort of paper tree can substitute the *papyrus romanus.*

485. **J. A. Martins. Province of Paraná.** BARKS and LEAVES of the Eucalyptus giganteus.

486. Commission General for the National Exhibitions. Rio de Janeiro. Samples of CAOUTCHOUC, from the Province of Rio Grande do Norte.

Samples of CAOUTCHOUC, from the Province of Amazonas.

NOTE.—This caoutchouc is a product of the *latex* of the *Siphonia elastica*, Pers. (*Hevea guyaneusis*). The exportation of caoutchouc from the Province of Amazonas amounts annually to 4,000,000 of kilogrammes, i. e. nearly the double of the exportation of same product extracted from the *Ticus elastica* in East Indies.

The Province of Amazonas exports also the "Brêo de Macaranduba (*Mimusopsetata*, considered as the true *gutta percha*.

Samples of CAOUTCHOUC, from the Province of Pará.

Samples of WAX and GUM of the "Carnaúba tree" from the Province of Rio Grande do Norte.

Samples of RESINS, from the Province of Minas Geraes.

487. Commission for the Province of Ceará. Sample of WAX, from Carnaúba tree. (Bot. *Copernicea cerifera, Mart.*)

NOTE.—This wax is advantageously used in Brazil for the manufacture of candles and domestic uses.

Samples of CAOUTCHOUC, from Mangabeira. (Bot. *Hancornia speciôsa.*)

NOTE.—This sort of Caoutchouc is an excellent substitute for the best quality of India Rubber.

488. J. F. Andrade Brant. Province of Minas Geraes. Samples of RESINS.

489. Commission for the District of Macáu. Province of Rio Grande do Norte. Samples of CAOUTCHOUC of "*Mangabeira*" tree. (Bot. *Ancornia speciosa.*)

NOTE.—This sort of *gum elastic* has been esteemed as one of the best in the opinion of the judges at Vienna Exhibition, and its cost does not exceed 50 cents a pound.

WAX of Carnaúba, (Bot. *Coryphecerifera.*)

NOTE.—The Carnaúba wax is esteemed very highly for manufacturing, and has been compared by Professor Toller, of Vienna, to the wax of Japan.

490. **Commission for the Province of "Rio Grande do Norte."** Various BALSAMS, generally employed for domestic uses.

491. **The Presidency of the Province of Goyaz.** RESIN of Cajueiro. (Bot. *Anachardium accidentale*). Highly esteemed for its medicinal properties.

492. **Commission for the Province of Goyaz.** RESIN of Mil-Homens. (Bot. *Aristolochia speciosa.*) Highly esteemed for its medicinal properties.

RESIN of Almacega. (Bot. *Icica Icicariba,*) esteemed also for medicinal and industrial properties, and known in Europe under the name of *elemi*.

493. **Lieutenant Colonel Sardinha. Province of Goyaz.** RESIN of the Pine tree, esteemed highly for its industrial and medicinal properties.

494. **Commission for the District of "Quebranguelo." Province of Alagôas.** RESIN of Angico. (Bot. *Acacia angicö,*) substitute of the *äcacia arabica, Lin.*

RESIN elemi. (Bot. *Icica.Icicariba.*)
RESIN of Jatobá. (Bot. *Hymænea courbaril.*)
RESIN of Ucunba. (Bot. *Myristica.*)

495. **T. R. da Silva. Province of Alagôas.** RESIN of Cajueiro. (Bot. *Anachardium occidentale.*)

RESIN of Mangabeira (*Ancornia speciosa.*)

496. **Commission for the District of Principe. Province of Rio Grande do Norte.** RESIN of *Pao Pereira*, largely used for lighting purposes.

> NOTE.—The *Pao Pereira* from Rio de Janeiro is classified as the "*Geissospernium Zellosie*;" but that of the Northern Provinces belongs to the genus *Aspidospserma*.

497. **Drs. J. C. da S. Muricy, etc. H. de Leaõ, Province of Paraná.** PINE-TREE BALSAM (Araucaria brasiliensis).

498. **F. P. Azevedo Portugal. Province of Paraná.** Samples of PINE TREE BALSAM.

499. D. F. Yellez, Perdigão. Province of Maranhão. Samples of RESIN Cajueiro. (Bot. *Anachardium accidentale.*)

500. Commission for the Province of Sancta Catharina. Samples of RESINS.

501. Gandeneio da Costa. Province of Parà. Samples of CAOUTCHOUC.

502. Commission for the Province of Pernumbuco. Samples of GUMS.

503. Felix Safarana. WAX ON THE BRANCH.

504. Commission for Acari. Provine of Rio Grande do Nàste. RESIN Benzoin. (Bot. *Styrax benzoin.*)

NOTE.—The Benzoin is an aromatic resin, highly esteemed for its medicinal virtues, being a powerful stimulant and tonic, and also as a precious ingredient in perfumery. It abounds on the mountains of the districts of "Serideé," "Pào dos Ferros," and Majoridade.

CLASS 605.

505. Cömmission for the Province of Ceará. BERRIES OF MAMONA. (Bot. *Ricinus-coummunis : fam. Euphorbiac_as.*)

506. Commission for the Province of Amazonas. SEEDS OF MAÇACOACAN, (Bot. *Theboroma ?*

NOTE.—Those seeds can be used as a good substitute for cacao.

SEEDS OF COCAO (*from Theobroma cacoa fruit or berry. Fam. of Bitnereaceas.*)

NOTE.—Those seeds are largely used as a basis in the preparation of *Chocolate* and of agreeable liquors; 1000 plants of Theobroma cacao produce approximately 1000 kilogrammes of fruits or berries during the space of 80 years.

507. D. Rosalina Paes Leme. Province of Sancta Catharina. Samples of LINSEED. (Bot. *Linum-uritatissimum.*)

508. Commission for the Province of Pará. Samples of NUTS.

509. Commission General for the National Exhibitions. Rio de Janeiro. DRY COCOANUTS, from Pernambuco.

BRAZILIAN NUTS (Castanhas), from the Province of Pará.

510. Dr. E. de Leão. Province of Paranà. COQUILHOS DE BUTIA. (Nuts of Butia. Bot. *Ænocarpus bacaba Martius.*)

AGRICULTURAL PRODUCTS.

CEREALS, GRASSES, AND FORAGE-PLANTS.

CLASS 620.

511. Commission General for the National Exhibitions. Rio de Janeiro.
Samples of HULLED and UNHULLED RICE, from the Province of Ceará.

Samples of YELLOW and COMMON CORN, from the same Province.

512. Commission for the Province of Paraná. Samples of WHEAT, RYE, OATS, and LINSEED.

513. Commission for the District of Lages. Province of Sancta Catharina. Samples of various CEREALS.

514. Commission for the Province of Maranhaõ. Samples of HULLED RICE.

515. Commission for the District of "Paulo Affonso." Province of Alagóas. CARNAUBA STRAW.

516. Colony of Sancta Maria da Soledade. Province of S. Pedro do Sul. Samples of RYE, OATS, and BARLEY.

517. Dr. J. C. S. Muricy. Province of Paraná. FENO PE DE GALLINHA. (Hay, called Hen's foot hay.)

518. Drs. E. D. Leaõ & S. Muricy. Province of Paraná. Samples of WHEAT and BARLEY.

Samples of HULLED and UNHULLED RICE.

519. Dr. E. de Leaõ. Province of Paraná. OATS on the straw.
RYE wheat on the straw.
Rich collection of samples of WHEAT, BARLEY, OATS, and MILLET.

520. **J. M. Leite Sampaio. Propriá, Province of Sergipe.** Samples of HULLED RICE.

521. **J. M. Leite. Propriá. Province of Sergipe.** Samples of HULLED and UNHULLED RICE.

522. **M. A. Guimarães. Paranagua, Province of Paraná.** Samples of various CEREALS. HULLED and UNHULLED RICE.

523. **Cordeira Gomes. Province of Paraná.** Samples of UNHULLED RICE.

524. **J. C. de Mello. Province of Ceará.** Samples of RICE SAQUAREMA.

525. **J. S. Aranjo. Province of Paraná.** CORN LEAVES, used for wrapping Cigarrettes.

526. **J. Olinto Mendes. Province of Paraná.** Collection of samples of CORN.

527. **B. Rocha Carvalho Iguape. Province of S. Paulo.** RICE of the first quality.

528. **Frederico Ritchert. Rio Grande, Province of S. Pedro do Sul.** CEREALS.

529. **A. Bento de Souza. Passo Fundo, Province of S. Pedro do Sul.** Samples of WHEAT.

530. **Schamalake. Province of Paraná.** HAY of *capin apurn*.

531. **M. Schiffer. Province of Paraná.** RYE and BARLEY.

532. **M. Schiffer & Schamalake. Province of Paraná.** BARLEY on the straw.

533. **J. A. Martins. Province of Paraná.** Samples of CANARY SEEDS. BARLEY.

534. **R. J. Ferreira Valle. Province of Maranhaõ.** Samples of UNHULLED RICE.

535. **Commission for the Province of Pará.** Samples of BARLEY.

536. **N. N.** Samples of MAIZE on the cob : CARNAUBA STRAW.

537. **Municipi of Lage. Province of Sancta Catharina.** Samples of WHEAT.

LEGUMINOUS PLANTS AND ESCULENT VEGETABLES.

CLASS 621.

538. Commission General for the National Exhibitions. Rio de Janeiro. BEANS and MARROWFAT BEANS, from the Province of Ceará.

539. Drs. C. Muricy & E. de Leaõ. Province of Paraná. Rich and varied collection of BEANS and other ESCULENTS.

540. Viscount de Jaguary. Province of Rio de Janeiro. ROSE BEANS, very abundant in that Province.

541. Commission for the District of "Guebranguelo. Province of Alagoãs. BEANS and GUANDU. (Bot. *Cajanus Flavus.*)
NOTE.—This Guandu is an edible and considered also as one of the best fertilizers.

542. A. F. de Moura. Province of Paraná. POTATOES.

MEDICINAL PLANTS AND ESCULENT VEGETABLES.

CLASS 621.

543. Commission General for the National Exhibitions. Rio de Janeiro. Collection of MEDICINAL PLANTS, from the Province of Amazonas, namely: PUXURI. (*Nectandria puxuri.*)
NOTE.—Powerful and aromatic stimulant; and the most efficaceous against *Cholera Morbus.*
GUARANA. (*Paulina sarlilis.*)
GUACO. (Bot. *Abithana guaco.*)
CAFERANA. (Bot. *Tacnia guyamensis.*)
BUTUA. (Bot. *Cisampelous-parreira.*)
SALSAPARRILHA. (*Smilax-salsaparrilha*). And many others.
NOTE.—The Salsaparrilha of Amazonas is the best in the markets, giving from 33 to 41 per cent. of extract,—while that of Vera Cruz (Mexico) only gives from 18 to 20 per cent.

544. (*b*) Collection of Medicinal Plants from the Province of Paraná.

545. (*c*) Collection of Medicinal Plants from the Province of Ceará.

546. (*d*) Samples of the Quinina Barks from the Province of Matto Grasso.

547. Commission for the City of Goyaz. Province of Goyaz. Collection of MEDICINAL PLANTS.

548. Commission for the Province of Cearà. Collection of MEDICINAL PLANTS.

549. Commision for the Province of S. Paulo. MEDICINAL BARKS.

550. Commission for the Province of Paraná. Collection of MEDICINAL PLANTS.

551. Commission for the Province of Goyaz. MEDICINAL PLANTS.

552. Commission for the District of Votuverava. Province of Parná. MEDICINAL PLANTS.

553. J. Lourenco. Correã. S. Paulo. MEDICINAL PLANTS.

554. G. de Souza Freitas. S. Paulo. Samples of MEDICINAL PLANTS.

555. A. J. Rodriguez d'Araujo. Rio de Janeiro. Samples of MEDICINAL PLANTS. (Comprehending nearly 40 different kinds.)

556. J. P. de Souza. Aranjo. Province of Paraná. MEDICINAL PLANTS, viz:—los on absynthio, (Bot. *Artemesia absinthiam,*) Maroica branco, (Bot. *Marrubiune americanum,*) Salsa korteuse, (Ap. *Petrosilinum,*) and Seeds of the Apple Tree.

557. Dr. A. J. de Carvalho. Province of S. Paulo. MEDICINAL PLANTS.

558. Theophilo do Fouseca. Province of S. Paulo. MEDICINAL PLANTS.

559. L. Tebiriçá Piratininga. Province of S. Paulo. MEDICINAL PLANTS.

560. Z. M. Foggia. Province of Goyaz. Collection of MEDICINAL PLANTS, viz:—of sucopira (*Borvdichia sp,*) *barks of quinine,* (*Strychnos pseudo, quina St. Hil,*) and tubers "Amaro Leite," (*Piptostegia Pissonis.*)

561. Norberto Barbósa. Province of Paraná. Collection of MEDICINAL PLANTS, viz:—Tauchagene (*Plantago, major,*) Alecrim (*Rosmarinus officinalis*), Herva Cidreira (*Mellissa off,*) Picãon Gerambû (*Bidens pillosa,*) Flôr de Barragem (*B. officinalis,*) Flôr de Sabuguerio (*Sambucus australis,*) Macella do Campo (*Conysa sp.*) and Aipo.

562. J. F. Guimarães. Province of Paraná. Collection of MEDICINAL PLANTS, viz:—Agrimonia (*Agrimonia eupatoria,*) Malva (*M. rotondifolia*), Mentrasto (*Cacalia mentrasto,*) Manduoirana (?) Andendro (*An graveoleus.*)

563. C. Falcão Dias. Province of Alagôas. MEDICINAL PLANTS.

564. Dr. F. A. d'Azevedo. Province of Goyaz. MEDICINAL PLANTS, viz:—Guaiaco (*guaiacum officinalis,*) Barks of Quinquina (*chinchona cuybensis* (?) Barks of Pào Pereira (*Geiss Vellosier,*) de Sancto Ignacio, (*Feuillea Trilobata.*)

565. Dr. J. J. s'Albuquer que Barros. Province of Cearà. Rich and varied collection of MEDICINAL PLANTS, comprehending 37 to 40 different sorts of plants, namely:—Barks of "Araroeira" (*Schinas terebinthifolius,*) Maxixe bravo (*Datura arborea*) considered as a specific against Asthma leaves, flowers and seeds of the caninana tree (*Chiococca,*) esteemed as a specific against dropsy, as well as a diuretic and diaphorestic parreira brava ou ruti (*Cissamplos parreira*) esteemed as a tonic and febrifuge, and also as an antidote to the *curare*, &c.

566. Dr. J. C. da Silva Muricy. Province of Paraná. MEDICINAL PLANTS.

567. M. E. do Sz Athayde. Province of Paranà. ALMACEGA. (*Icica Icicariba,*) and Poia do Compo (*Polygala poaya*, Mart.)

568. A. Philippe. Province of Paranà. TEARS OF THE VIRGIN, highly esteemed for its medicinal virtues, Para tudo "Good for all," There are different plants known in Brazil under this same name viz: 1. "Para tudo," or a *Winterianea canella*, fam. of the guttiferas, 2. An amarantacea, i. e. the Gamphrena officinalis, Mart.

ROOTS AND TUBERS.

CLASS 622.

569. J. F. Andrade Brant. Province of Minas Geraes. MEDICINAL ROOTS.

570. Dr. Heredia de Sá. Campos, Province of Rio de Janeiro. HEREDIA ROOT (a discovery of the exhibitor.)

571. Commission for the Province of Paraná. MANIOC TUBERS.

572. Commision for the Province of S. Paulo. MEDICINAL ROOTS.

573. Dr. Muricy. Province of Paraná. SWEET FLAG. (Bot. *Calamus*.)

TOBACCO, HOPS TEA, COFFEE, AND SPICES.

SPICES.

CLASS 623.

574. Commission General for the National Exhibitions. Rio de Janeiro.

(*a*) Samples of CLOVE, (Bot. *Dicypellium Cayrophyllatum; cloves aromaticus*), from the Province of Amazonas.

NOTE.—This sort of clove is remarkable for its fine aroma, and is largely employed in domestic and medicinal uses.

(*b*) GINGER (Bot. *Zingiber officinalis*), from the Province of Pará.

NOTE.—This ginger is largely used for medicinal purposes.

(*c*) VANILLA (Bot. *Baunilla*), from the Province of Matto Grosso.

(*d*) VANILLA, from the locality called "Morro do Chapéu," Province of Bahia.

575. **Commission for the Capital of the Province of Goyaz.** GINGER, SAFFRON, VANILLA.

576. **Municipality of Cametá. Province of Para.** Samples of CACAO.

577. **J. M. d'Araujo Triste. Province of Paraná.** CLOVES OF INDIA. (Bot. *Coriophylus aromaticus.*)

578. **Dr. Richter. Colony of Mont 'Alverne, Province of S. Pedro do Sul**
WHITE MUSTARD. (Bot. *Sinapis alba*).
BLACK MUSTARD. (Bot. *Sinapis nigra*).

579. **M. A. Guimarães & Rev. J. H. Pedrozo. Province of Paraná.**
VANILLA AROMATICA.

580. **F. Fernandes Portella. Province of Pernambuco.** VANILLA.

581. **J. F. d'Andrade Brant. Province of Minas Geraes.** Samples of VANILLA.

582. **A. de Padua G. Province of Goyaz.** VANILLA.

583. **M. C. Silva & Filhos, Lage. Province of Rio de Janeiro.** Samples of CACAO.

584. **L. F. do Pinho. Rio de Janeiro.** Samples of various sorts of CHOCOLATE, viz. :
PULVERIZED CHOCOLATE (*soluvel em po*).
MOSS CHOCOLATE (*chocolate de musgo*).
HOMŒOPATHIC CHOCOLATE (*Homœopathico*).
CINNAMON CHOCOLATE (*chocolate de canella*).
VANILLA CHOCOLATE (*chocolate de baunilha*).

585. **Dias Lima. S. Salvador da Bahia.** Samples of CHOCOLATE.

586. **J. A. F. Ribeiro. S. Luiz, Province of Maranhão.** Samples of CHOCOLATE.

587. **Commission for the Province of S. Paulo.** Samples of CHOCOLATE.

588. **Liborio & Ferreira. Province of S. Paulo.** Samples of CHOCOLATE.

589. Dr. Agostinho E. de Leaõ. Province of Paraná.
(*a*) GINGER. (Bot. *Zingiber officinalis*).
NOTE.—This Ginger is esteemed as a powerful stimulant and a preventative against cholera-morbus.
(*b*) Samples of odoriferous PEPPER. (Bot. *capsicum odoriferum*).

590. Dr. J. C. da Silva Muricy. Province of Paraná. BAUNILHA (*Vanilla aromatica*).

COFFEE.*

591. Commission for the Province of Ceará. Samples of LEAD COLOURED COFFEE (*cafe chumbado*).
NOTE.—This coffee substitutes in the European markets the coffee of "La-Guayra."

592. Commission for the Province of Maranhão. Samples of HULLED and UNHULLED COFFEE (*cafe em casca e socado*).
NOTE.—This coffee is considered of a good quality.
Samples of common COFFEE.

593. Commission for the Province of Sergipe. Samples of COFFEE.

594. Commission for the Province of Parahyba do Nórte, Samples of COFFEE.

595. The Presidency of the Province of Santa Catharina. Samples of COFFEE.
NOTE.—The cultivation of coffee was commenced a few years ago in the Province of Sancta Catharina, and has proven very successful.

596. Baron de Araguara. Araguara, Province of S. Paulo. Samples of COFFEE.

---

* NOTE.—Coffee is actually esteemed as the best product and as the first cause of the public wealth in Brazil. The coffee plants grows there every where, and the exportation of coffee during the period from July 1873, to July 1874, amounted to 172,449,797 kilogrammes, representing a value of nearly 50 millions dollars.

AGRICULTURAL PRODUCTS. 79

597. **J. J. Franco Falcão.** Fazenda do Frade, Province of Rio de Janeiro.
COFFEE.

598. **J. F. da Nobrega So.** Pirahy, Province of Rio de Janeiro. COFFEE.

599. **F. C. de Magalhães.** Cantagollo, Province of Rio de Janeiro.
COFFEE.

600. **A. de Sá Albuquerque.** Muribeca, Province of Pernambuco.
COFFEE.

601. **Pedro J. de Lima.** Province of Bahia. COFFEE.

602. **A. F. de Lacerda.** Province of Bahia. COFFEE.

603. **L. de Sz Breves.** Province of Minas Geraes. COFFEE.

604. **J. J. de Sz Breves.** Piraky, Province of Rio de Janeiro. COFFEE.

605. **Baron de Sz Gueiroz.** Province of S. Paulo. COFFEE.

606. **J. F. de Paula Souza.** Province of S. Paulo. COFFEE.

607. **A. S. de Miranda Jordão.** Bempósta, Province of Rio de Janeiro.
COFFEE.

608. **P. M. da Cósta.** Province of Minas Geraes. COFFEE.

609. **Viscount de Jaguary.** Trez-Barras, Province of Rio de Janeiro.
Samples of COFFEE, dried and decorticated by different processes.
NOTE.—The washed coffee is decorticated by American machines. The common coffee (cafê de Terreiro) is gathered in sieves, sun dried, decorticated and polished by American machines.

610. **D. Maria, C. J. Silva & Filhos.** Lage, Province of Rio de Janeiro.
Samples of decorticated and sun dried COFFEE.

611. **Viscountess do Rio Noao.** Rio Noao. Province of Rio de Janeiro.
COFFEE.

612. Baron da Bella Vista. Bananal. Province of S. Paulo. Samples of hulled or decorticated COFFEE of the years 1874 and 1875. Samples of sun dried COFFEE of the year 1874. Washed and sun dried COFFEE of the year 1875.

NOTE.—The coffee of S. Paulo (which is exported through " Santos,") enjoys the best reputation in the foreign markets, and there are few farmers of S. Paulo who do not employ machinery for improving coffee.

613. Baron de Camargos. Province of Minas Geraes. COFFEE.

614. Baron de Juparanà & Comp. Sancta Monica. Province of Rio de Janeiro. COFFEE.

615. Viscount de Prados. Province of Minas Geraes. COFFEE.

616. Councillor Carrão. Province of S. Paulo. COFFEE.

617. Commandeur Montenegro. Nova Lousã. Province of S. Paulo. COFFEE.

618. Baron de Atibaia. Province of S. Paulo. COFFEE.

619. Colonel J. Pinto Tavares. Parahyba do Sul. Province of Rio de Janeiro. COFFEE, sun-dried.

620. P. J. Monteiro. Rio de Janeiro. COFFEE.

621. J. T. M. Portella. Province of Pernambuco. COFFEE from Muribéca.

622. Dezembargadõr Gaveaõ. S. Bernardo. Province of S. Paulo. COFFEE.

623. J. R. dos Sanctos Camargo. Province of S. Paulo. COFFEE.

624. Luiz Bornaud. Caravellas. Province of Bahia. Samples of round and chosen COFFEE.

625. M. de Freitas Lemos. Rio de Janeiro. Samples of hulled and polished COFFEE.

626. Silverio R. Jordão. Province of S. Paulo. COFFEE.

627. F. L. d'Almeida Magalhães. Fazenda do Triumpho. Province of Rio de Janeiro. COFFEE.

AGRICULTURAL PRODUCTS. 81

628. **C. J. Fernandes. Maragogipe. Province of Bahia.** Samples of COFFEE, remarkable for the peculiar size of the berry.

   NOTE.—This coffee has been found in the forests of the Province of Bahia, as affirms the exhibitor, and is now cultivated on his plantation.

629. **A. Cornelio dos Santos. Fazendo de S. Roque. Province of Rio de Janeiro.** Samples of peeled and sun-dried COFFEE.

630. **Domingos G. Jardim. Cidade de Rezendo. Province of Rio de Janeiro.** Samples of SUN DRIED COFFEE.

631. **M. Antonio Airósa. Cantagallo. Province of Rio de Janeiro.** Five samples of superior COFFEE, viz :—*Washed or peeled Coffee, Sun dried Coffee, Moka Coffee, Unhulled Coffee, Coffee em casquinha.*

   NOTE.—These samples are equal to those sent by the Exhibitor to the foreign markets.

632. **J. L. Belens. Fazenda do Macaco. Province of Rio de Janeiro.** COFFEE.

633. **N. A. Claudio Reines. Monte Vernon. Province of Rio de Janeiro.** COFFEE.

634. **F. Marcondes Machado. Porto Novo do Cunha. Province of Rio de Janiero.** COFFEE.

635. **J. J. Alves da Cunha. S. Fidelis. Province of Rio de Janeiro.** Samples of Superior COFFEE.

636. **Fribourg & Filhos. Cantagallo. Province of Rio de Janeiro.** Samples of various sorts of COFFEE.

   NOTE.—This coffee has such a high reputation tnat it is not sent to market.

637. **J. Nobrega d'Oliveira. Bõa Esperança. Province of Rio de Janeiro.** COFFEE.

638. **A. B. Cósta Pereira. Fazenda da Piedade. Province of Rio de Janeiro.** COFFEE.

639. **Umbelino Tosta. Cachoeira. Province of Bahia.** Samples of hulled and unhulled COFFEE.

640. **F. A. F. de Azevedo. Province of Goyaz.** Samples of washed and sun-dried COFFEE.

641. V. Moretti Toggia. Province of Goyaz. COFFEE, washed and sun-dried.

642. J. de Assis Alves. Province of Minas Ceraes. COFFEE.

643. M. d'Aguiar Valim. Bananal. Province of S. Paulo. COFFEE.

644. J. M. Freire. Province of S. Paulo. Sun dried COFFEE.

645. José Vergueiro. Ibicaba. Province of S. Paulo. COFFEE.

646. M. B. de Siqueira. Meia Ponte. Province of S. Paulo. COFFEE.

647. J. T. A. Nogueira. Province of S. Paulo. COFFEE.

648. Dr. P. R. Nogueira. Province of S. Paulo. COFFEE.

659. L. Teixeira de Barros. Pindamonhangaba. Province of S. Paulo. Sun dried and polished COFFEE.

650. Raphael A. P. de Barros. Province of S. Paulo. COFFEE.

651. L. A. de Souza Barros. Province of S. Paulo. COFFEE.

652. Ant. P. do Amaral. Province of S. Paulo. COFFEE.

653. Francisco P. do Amaral. Province of S. Paulo. COFFEE.

654. D. Maria T. do Amaral. Campinas. Province of S. Paulo. COFFEE.

655. Frederika Krull. Caravellas. Province of Bahia. Samples of common, hulled and decorticated COFFEE.

COFFEE-HULLS, roasted and pulverised.

NOTE.—The coffee-hulls are employed as a substitute for coffee berries.

656. A. E. C. Iguape. Province of S. Paulo. COFFEE.

657. F. N. Calmon Nogueira da Gama. Valença. Province of Rio de Janeiro. COFFEE.

658. E. N. Togueira da Gama. Province of Rio de Janeiro. COFFEE.

659. Manuel da Rocha Leaõ. Resende. Province of Rio de Janeiro. Samples of various sorts of COFFEE, viz :—Sun dried COFFEE, Decorticated COFFEE, yellow coloured COFFEE, Round or Moka COFFEE.

NOTE.—All these sorts of Coffee are equal to those sent to the foreign markets, and esteemed in Europe as the best.

TOBACCO.

660. Commission for the town of "Fortaleza." Province of Ceará.
SNUFF, prepared by Paes Pinto & Son.

661. Commission for the town of Cuyabà. Province of Matto Grosso.
TOBACCO LEAVES, CIGARS.

662. Commission for the Province of Amazonas. TOBACCO prepared with the leaves of the *Nicotiana-tabacum*, of the family "Solanaceas."
NOTE.—This tobacco is esteemed one of the best qualities.

663. Commission for the Province of Ceará. Samples of TOBACCO.

664. Commission for the Province of Maranhaõ. TOBACCO in rolls.

665. Commission for the Province of Goyaz. CIGARETTES, with corn-straw wrappers.
NOTE.—The tobacco from the Province of Goyaz is highly esteemed in the market of Rio de Janeiro. From July 1873, to July 1874, that Province exported 9,478 kilogr. of tobàcco, representing a value (official) of nearly three thousand dollars.

666. Commission for the Province of Paraná. Samples of TOBACCO.
NOTE.—Tobacco grows well in this Province, but more especially at the following places: "Assunguy," "Tibagy," "Paranápanema," "Ignassú" and "Ivanhy" where the temperature is higher.

667. Commission for the Municipe of "Paulo Affonso," Province of Alagoãs. SPUN TOBACCO.

668. Commission for the District of "Mõrro do Chapèu, Province of Bahia. Samples of SPUN TOBACCO.

669. Colony of Assunguy, Província of Paraná. TOBACCO LEAVES.

670. Colony of Itajahy, Province of Sancta Catharina. LEAF TOBACCO, [superior.]

671. Director of the Colony, Sancta Maria do Soledade, Province of S. Pedro do Sul. TOBACCO LEAVES.

672. Presidency of the Province of Bahia.   S. Salvador da Bahia.
CIGARS of different shapes.

NOTE.—The cigars from Bahia are the most reputed in Brazil, and when well prepared compete with the Havana cigars.

673. Pereira & Braga.   Rio de Janeiro. CIGARS.

NOTE.—The Exhibitors have a large establishment, and the quality as well as the amount of their product shows its developement.

674. J. R. dos Santos, Camargo.   Province of S. Paulo. LEAF TOBACCO, and samples of HAVANA TOBACCO, cultivated by the exhibitor.

NOTE.—The tobacco from S. Paulo is very much esteemed in the markets. The tobacco exported by that Province from 1871 to 1874, amounted to 2,428,582 kilogr.

675. D. Rosalina V. Paes Leme.   Province of Sancta Catharina. CIGARS made at the Colony of Blumenau.

TOBACCO, from the same Colony.

SPUN TOBACCO from Lages.

676. Factory of S. João de Nictheroy.   Province of Rio de Janeiro.
CIGARETTES with paper wrappers.

Samples of TOBACCO, prepared for pipes and cigarettes.

677. Dr. Silva Muricy.   Province of Paraná. Samples of TOBACCO.
CIGARETTES, corn straw wrapped.

CIGARS made by the *Bugres* (Indians) of Guarapava.

678. Fr. d'Assis C. Moreira.   Codó, Province of Maranhão. LEAF TOBACCO.

679. Souza Queiroz & Filhos.   Province of S. Paulo. SPUN TOBACCO.

680. Salamon Levy.   Teffé, Province of Amazonas. SNUFF.

681. João Schild.   Colony Sancta Cruz, Province of S. Pedro do Sul. CIGARS.

682. August Herbst.   Colony of Blumenau, Province of Sancta Catharina. SPUN TOBACCO.

683. **Guilherme Rosenstock.** **Colony of Joinville, Province of Sancta Catharina.** TOBACCO.

684. **Christiano Kopsch.** **Colony of Blumenau, Province of Sancta Catharina.** TOBACCO.

685. **Maxim Merck.** **Colony of Blumenau, Province of Sancta Catharina.** TOBACCO.

686. **Vander Berg.** **Colony of, Sancta Cruz, Province of S. Pedro do Sul.** TOBACCO SEEDS and LEAVES.

> NOTE.—The ex-colony of Sancta Cruz is one of the richest parts of the Province, regarding the production of tobacco. There are in this ex-colony nearly nine thousand inhabitants, and its exportation of tobacco amounts to ten thousand bags a year.

687. **Dr. F. Richter.** **Province of S. Pedro do Sul.** TOBACCO, from the Colony Sancta Emilia.

LEAF TOBACCO, from the Colony Mount Alverne.

688. **Carlos Seidler.** **Colony of Sancta Cruz.** **Province of S. Pedro do Sul.** LEAF TOBACCO.

689. **Barron de Kalden.** **Colony of Sancto Angelo, Province of S. Pedro do Sul.** LEAF TOBACCO.

690. **Henrique Ketterman.** **Colony of Soncto Angelo, Province of S. Pedro do Sul.** LEAF TOBACCO.

691. **Augusto Dietrich.** **Colony of Joinville, Province of Sancta Catharina.** LEAF TOBACCO.

692. **Mel. Pinto Figueredo.** **Itabapoana, Province of Rio de Janeiro.** SPUN TOBACCO, prepared in stoves.

693. **F. Espindola da Veiga.** **Rio de Janeiro.** TOBACCO, (first quality.)

694. **Bellarmino de Faria.** **Province of Bahia.** TOBACCO, prepared for pipes and cigarette use.

695. **Fr. Luiz da Grava.** **Cachveira, Province of Bahia.** SAMPLES OF TOBACCO.

696. **M. B. de Siqueira.** **Meia Ponte, Province of Goyaz.** ROLLED TOBACCO.

AGRICULTURAL PRODUCTS.

697. Pinto & Irmãos. Nazareth, Province of Bahia. SAMPLES OF TOBACCO.

698. J. Z. de Louza. Bakiaua, Province of Bahia. SAMPLES OF TOBACCO.

699. J. D. Aranha. Province of S. Paulo. Samples of a sort of TOBACCO called (*Fumo Georgino*).

700. Ernesto A. Ferreira. Barbacena, Province of Minas Geraes. CIGARETTES, straw wrapped.

701. Candido J. Ferreira. Cachoeira, Province of Bahia. CIGARS.

702. D. de Rocka Ferreira. Municipe da Pomba, Province of Minas Geraes. Rolled TOBACCO (superior quality.)

NOTE: Mr. D. de Racha Ferreira, is one of the best manufacturers of tobacco, and well known in the Brazilian and foreign markets. Price $2 50 per pound.

703. Domingos V. Paraiso. Cidäde de Itu, Province of S. Paulo. Carolino TOBACCO.

704. F. Viotti. Baependy, Province of Minas Geraes. Samples of TOBACCO, rolled and curled.

705. Cerqueira & Comp. S. Salvador da Bahia. SNUFF (Princeza Imperial).
CIGARS and CIGARETTES.

706. M. J. de Mendonça. "Meia Ponte," Province of Oayaz. Rolled TOBACCO.

707. J. E. Pinheiro. Bragança, Province of Pará. TOBACCO.

708. Rev. Marcellino de Menezes. Ourem, Province of Pará. TOBACCO.

709. J. R. de Moraes Jardim. Jaraguá, Province of Goyaz. TOBACCO.

710. Rev. A. F. do Nascimento. Province of Goyaz. TOBACCO of a sort called in Brazil "Tobacco Jorge Pequeno."

711. J. C. Panitz. S. Leopoldo, Province of S. Pedro do Sul. TOBACCO.

NOTE.—This tobacco is manufactured and pressed in the same manner as the tobacco of the United States, and competes in quality with that one.

712. **Nuno B. de Senna.** Mucury, Province of Minas Geraes. Rolled TOBACCO.

713. **M. A. dos Santos.** Colony of Blumenau. Province of Sancta Catharina. BAILED TOBACCO.

714. **P. Coelho d'Oliveira.** Municipe da Pomba, Province of Minas Geraes. TOBACCO.

715. **A. Ignacio da Silva.** Limoeiro. Province of Alagôas. ROLLED TOBACCO.

716. **J. Constantino.** Baependy, Province of Rio de Janeiro. Samples of TOBACCO, first quality, spun and curled.

717. **M. L. de Souza.** Province of Paraná. CIGARETTES.

718. **Rev. C. J. R. de Souza.** Aveiros. Province of Pará. TOBACCO.

719. **Umbelino Tasta.** Nazareth. Province of Bahia. Samples of TOBACCO.

720. **J. L. Sá Ribas.** Province of Paraná. SPUN TOBACCO.

721. **E. Cohin.** Aveiros Province of Pará. SPUN TOBACCO.

722. **J. Pinto Gohsalves.** Province of S. Paulo. CIGARS.

723. **T. J. Souza Gama.** Ovro-Preto, Province of Minas Geraes. CIGARS.

724. **H. Guedes.** S. Salvador da Bahia. Choice CIGARS.

725. **J. Monteiro d'Abreu.** Province of S. Paulo. CIGARS.

726. **Nestor M. Borba.** Assunguy, Province of Paraná. CIGARETTES, corn straw wrapped and covered with tobacco leaves, manufactured at the colony of Assunguy.

727. **Vasconcellos & Filhos.** Province of Ceará. CIGARETTES of various brands.

728. **J. Barbósa de Miranda.** Rio de Janeiro. CIGARETTES of various qualities.

729. **J. Dias Aranha.** Province of S. Paulo. CIGARETTES.

730. **F. D. Perneta.** Province of Paraná. CIGARETTES, straw wrapped.

731. **A. L. d'Andrade Ribas.** Province of S. Paulo. CIGARETTES straw wrapped.

732. **L. F. Ramos.** Ouro Preto, Province of Minas Geraes. CIGARETTES.

733. **J. Lepage.** Barbacena, Province of Minas Geraes. CIGARETTES.

734. **Dr. E. de Leão.** Province of Paraná. CIGARETTES, put together in the form of mattings.

735. **F. de S. C. Rocha.** Rio de Janeiro. SNUFF (Rapé Princeza da Bahia).

736. **J. Paulo Cordeiro.** Rio de Janeiro. Samples of seven qualities of SNUFF.
Pulverized SNUFF.

> NOTE.—The manufacture of snuff develops every day more and more in Brazil. There are already a great many varieties, owing to the different processes of preparation, and their exportation to the European markets increases every year.
>
> NOTE.—Price 50 cts. to $1 a pound.

737. **Vasconcellos & Filhos. Fortaleza, Province of Ceará.** IMPERIAL SNUFF (*Rapé Imperial*).

> NOTE.—This snuff competes with the best snuff manufactured in England, and is known under the name of Prince Albert's snuff.

TEA, MATTE.

738. **J. L. Martins. Fazenda do Paraiso.** Rio de Janeiro. NATIONAL TEA, (Thea Sinensis).

739. **F. A. Miranda Russo.** Province of S. Paulo. NATIONAL TEA

740. **Counsellor Carrão.** Province of S. Paulo. NATIONAL TEA.

741. **A. P. de Régo Freitas.** Province of S. Paulo. NATIONAL TEA.

742. **J Ribeiro Neves.** Province of S. Paulo. NATIONAL TEA.

743. **F. A. Galvão da França.** Province of S. Paulo. NATIONAL TEA.

744. J. Ribeiro Xavier. Province of S. Paulo. TEA.

NOTE.—Tea (*Thea Sinensis*) is largely cultivated in the Province of S. Paulo. That Province exports every year more than 100,000 kilogrammes, without mentioning the tea consumed in the interior.

745. A. L. M. Mosqueira, Camargos. Province of Minas Geraes. Samples of different brands of TEA.

746. T. P. Correa Anstomina. Province of Paraná. MATTE, (Special sort of Brazilian tea or holly,) *Bot. Ilex Paraguayensis.*

747. Ildefonso Correa. Province of Paraná. MATTE.

NOTE.---These samples of Matte have been prepared in the same way that is used to prepare it for exportation to Chili and the Republics of the Pacific.

748. Imperial Institute Fluminense d'Agriculture. TEA made of coffee leaves, and prepared in the same way as the India Tea, except the tortion.

NOTE: This sort of tea is esteemed as an excellent substitute for coffee.

749. Commission for the Province of Minas Geraes. Samples of MATTE.

750. Major V. F. de Leão. Province of Paraná. Samples of MATTE, prepared in different manners: in leaves, dried and twisted, or pulverized.

NOTE: The *Matte* is an excellent substitute for coffee and tea, and remarkably odoriferous, diuretic and nutritive. It contains the theine principle in larger quantities than coffee or tea. The Matte prepared in leaves is consumed in the northern Provinces; the pulverized Matte in the Provinces of Paraná and S. Pedro do Sul. Immense quantities of Pulverized Matte are also exported to the Republics of River Platte, the Argentine Confederation, and the Republic of Uruguay.

751. D. dos Santos Pacheco. Province of Paraná. MATTE LEAVES.

NOTE: This Matte is prepared in the same manner as tea.

752. J. M. da Silva Braga. Province of Paraná. MATTE in leaves.

753. G. d'A. Torres. Province of Paraná. MATTE.

754. **J. Bley. Province of Paraná.** MATTE.

755. **Ildefonso J. G. d'Andrade. Province of Paraná.** MATTE.

756. **Ribas d'Andrade. Province of Paraná.** MATTE.

757. **M. d'A. Torres. Province of Parana.** MATTE.

758. **J. d'Almeida Torres. Province of Parana.** MATTE.

759. **M. d'O. Cercal. Province of Paraná.** MATTE in leaves.

760. **L. M. Agnez. Province of Paraná.** Samples of MATTE—ordinary and fine pulverized. Samples of SENNA in leaves.

761. **C. J. Munhoz. Province of Paraná.** MATTE.

762. **P. P. Azevedo Portugal. Province of Paraná.** MATTE.

763. **Henrique Sepper. Colony of Joinville Co. Province of Sancta Catharina.** MATTE.

764. **D. Rosalina Paes Leme. Lages. Province of Sancta Catharina.** MATTE.

765. **A. de Paulo Xavier. Province of Paraná.** Matte.

766. **P. de Siqueira, Cortes. Province of Paraná.** MATTE.

767. **Tiburcio de Macedo. Province of Paraná.** MATTE.

NOTE: This Matte is specially to be exported to the Republic of Chili.

768. **João Diarson. Province of S. Pedro do Sul.** MATTE.

769. **A. Bento de Souza. Province of S. Pedro do Sul.** MATTE.

770. **A. Proost Rodovalho. Province of S. Paulo.** MATTE,

771. **Central Exportation Co.,** (Companhia Central de Exportação,) **Province of Paraná.** MATTE.

NOTE.—The Matte from the Province of Paranà is almost all of superior quality, and constitutes a most important branch of exportation. The amount of Mattè exported from 1873 to 1874 raised to 12,356,044 kilogr, representing a value of about one million dollars.

SPICES.

772. Commission General for the National Exhibitions. Rio de Jeneiro.
PINDAHIBA FRUITS (*Xilspia sericra*) from the Province of Alagoas.

NOTE.— These fruits substitute the Cayenne Pepper.

SEEDS AND SEED VESSELS.

CLASS 624.

773. Commission General for the National Exhibition. SEEDS OF CUMARU (Bot. *Dipterix cumaru vel odorata.*)

NOTE.—The cumaru seeds are remarkable for their fine aroma.

774. J. Lepage. Province of Minas Geraes. VARIOUS SEEDS.

775. Dr. Ermelindo de Leão. Province of Paraná. MATTIE SEEDS, (Bot. *Ilex Paraguayensis, Fam. Iliciniaceas*).

776. Drs. Ermelinde de Leão and Muricy. Province of Paraná. SEEDS OF PINE TREE.

777. Colony of Sancta Maria da Saledade. Province of S. Pedro do Sul. LINSEED, (Bot. *Linum uri tatissimum.*)

778. Dr. J. C. da Silva Muricy. Province of Paraná. SEEDS OF SUNFLOWER, (*Girasoli*. Bot. *Helianthus annuus.*)

NOTE: These seeds produce an excellent oil for table.

779. Perdigão. Province of Maranhão. BACURY SEEDS.

780. Commission for the Province of Alagoãs. VANILLA SEEDS and OTHER SEEDS.

781. Viscount de Faguary. Trez Barras. Province of Rio de Janeiro. SEEDS OF THE PALMA CHRISTI TREE.

LAND ANIMALS.

INSECTS—USEFUL AND INJURIOUS.

CLASS 638.

782. Dr. Nicolàu J. Moreira. Rio de Janeiro. BORBOLETA SERIGENICA, (a sort of Butterfly which produces silk.) *(Attacus Aurota Lepidopterous).*

Common name, Butterfly, "*Porta Espelhos.*"

Class,	Insects.
Order,	Lepidopterous.
Family,	Nosturnas.
Section,	Bombycianous.
Genus,	Attacus.
Subgenus,	Saturnia.
Species,	Aurota.

NOTE.—This Butterfly abounds in almost all the Empire of Brazil. It produces during each generation about 240 *cocoons* of silk; each *cocoon* weighing 2½ *drachms*, and producing 30 *grains* of fine silk. The fibre of a yellowish colour, is strong elastic, and long, a single thread sustains a weight of 4 drachms, and a cord of 24 threads resists the weight of ¾ of a pound. The "Larva" of this insect subsists on the leaves of "*Mamona*" (Bot. *Ricinus*), of Beribà (Bot. *Anona*) and principally on the "Cajazeiro" (Bot. *Spondias.*)

The great advantage in the cultivation of this Lepidopterous consists that the Butterfly enclosed in the cocoon can be preserved and utilized without breaking the fibre.

783. Luiz de Rezende. Rio de Janeiro. Collection of SILK WORMS from their first day until the formation of the cocoon, preserved in alcohol.

Collection of BUTTERFLIES.

784. Ernesto E. Wirmond. Province of Paranà. Collection of INSECTS.

ANIMAL AND VEGETABLE PRODUCTS.

(Used as Food or as Materials.)

THE DAIRY, MILK, CREAM, AND CHEESE.

CLASS 651.

785. **Commission General for the National Exhibition. Rio de Janeiro.** BUTTER of Tartle.

CHEESES prepared in different manners.

786. **Fr. Juliano. Province of Paraná.** CHEESE manufactured on the Italian system.

CHEESES.

787. **B. Rodriguez Carneiro. Province of Paraná** Brazilian CHEESES.

788. **Dr. Ubatuba. Rio Grande. Province of S. Pedro do Sul.** Condensed MILK.

789. **J. F. D. Cabral. Province of Alagoãs.** MILK of Mangabeira.

790. **M. G. de Moraes Sozeira. Province of Paroa.** Brazilian CHEESE.

791. **Dr. A. E. de Leaõ. Province of Paraná.** CHEESE prepared after the Italian system.

792. **Director of Paranàpanema. Province of Paraná.** Samples of BUTTER.

AGRICULTURAL PRODUCTS.

HIDES, FURS AND LEATHER, IVORY, BONE, ETC.

CLASS 652.

793. **Commission General for the National Exhibitions.** **Rio de Janeiro.**
   (*a*) Collection of SKINS of Animals, from Cuyaba. Province of Matto Grosso.
   (*b*) Panther SKINS and other hides from the Province of Goyaz.
   (*c*) Collection of SKINS of Animals, packed in straw, from the Province of Paranà.
   (*d*) HIDES and LEATHER, from the Province of Rio Grande do Nórte.
   (*e*) SKINS, HIDES and HORNS, from the Province of Matto Grosso.
   (*f*) SKINS of Animals from the Province of Alagoas.
   (*g*) SKINS of Animals, from the Province of Amazonas.
   (*h*) HIDES and LEATHER, from the Province of Cearà.

794. **Commission for the Province of Paranà.** OX-HORNS.
   Ox and STAG HORNS.
   HIDES and SKINS of various animals.

795. **Ignacio d'Oliveira. Goyaz.** GLUE in *laminas*.

796. **Commission for the District of "Principe. Province of Rio Grande do Nórte.** SKINS and HIDES of various animals.

797. **J. C. Paes d'Andrade. Irajà. Rio de Janeiro.** Samples of GLUE.

798. **D. M. P. S. Ubatuba. Rio de Janeiro.** Samples of TALLOW, LARD and OIL.

799. **D. F. Maciel. Province of Paranà.** SKINS of Steer.

800. **Colonel P. Cortez. Province of Paranà.** HIDE of a black steer.

801. **A. C. A. Botelho. Province of Paranà.** SKINS of Sucury (Boa aquatica).

802. **M. E. S. Athayde. Province of Paraná.** Various SKINS.

803. **F. D. Perneta. Province of Paraná.** Two STAG-HORNS.

804. **J. Feydel Filho. Rio de Janeiro.** Collection of HIDES, tanned and raw.

805. **I. J. Andrade. Province of Paraná.** Cow HIDES, and SKINS of steer (spotted).

806. **Commission for the Province of S. Paulo.** HIDES and LEATHER.

807. **Costa Eymoel & Co. Rio Grande. Province of S. Pedro do Sul.** HIDES, LEATHER and SOLE.

> NOTE.—The exhibitors are large manufacturers, and all the work is performed by machinery; their products compete favourably with similar imports from abroad.

808. **Klippel & Irmão. Trez. Forquihag. Province of S. Pedro do Sul.** HIDES and SOLES.

CLASS 654.

809. **Commission General for the National Exhibitions. Rio de Janeiro.** Samples of BEES-WAX, from the Province of Rio Grande do Norte.

Samples of yellow WAX, in cake and in laminas, from the Province of Paraná.

810. **D. Maria Miro. Province of Paraná.** Samples of yellow WAX, in cakes and in laminas.

811. **Rev. J. M. C. Araujo. Itadorahy. Province of Rio de Janeiro.** Samples of BEES-WAX.

812. **A. P. Safarana. Itaborahy. Province of Rio de Janeiro.** Samples of BEES-WAX and CANDLES.

813. **Commission for the Province of Goyaz.** Samples of BEES-WAX.

814. **Commission for the District of Principe. Province of Rio Grande do Norte.** BEES-WAX.

815. **J. Pereira de Sz. Araujo.** **Paraná.** Yellow WAX.

816. **J. A. Vioira d'Araujo.** **Paranàpanema.** **Province of Paraná.** Collection of bottles of HONEY.

817. **A. de Paula Xavier.** **Province of Paraná.** Samples of HONEY, bottled.

818. **D. Leocadia de P. Xavier.** **Province of Paraná.** Samples of WAX, yellow coloured.

819. **J. Olinto Mendes.** **Province of Paraná.** Samples of HONEY. Samples of BEES-WAX, yellow coloured.

820. **Long & Co.** Samples of WAX.

821. **Macedo & Azerido.** **Province of S. Pedro do Sul.** Samples of WAX, white and yellow coloured.

> NOTE.—The industry of wax has been so much developed during the last years, that now the Province of S. Pedro do Sul imports no more wax candles from foreign markets. The production is estimated to be actually thousands of thousands of kilogrammes a year, and the amount still increases.

PRESERVED MEATS, VEGETABLES, FRUITS, ETC.

CLASS 656.

822. **Commission General for the National Exhibitions, Rio de Janeiro.** MEATS preserved in jars, from the Province of Parà.

Preserved BEEF and dried TONGUES, from the Province of S. Pedro do Sul.

Origones, prepared with peaches, in the Province of Paraná.

823. **Commission for the Province of Ceará.** CONFECTIONERIES and samples of SUN-DRIED BEEF.

824. **Rosalina R. Botelho Canoza.** **Parà.** Preserved VEGETABLES.

825. **F. P. de Vasconcellos. S. Salvador da Bahia.** Preserved VEGETABLES AND BEANS.

826. **Gouthiere and Wagner. Rio de Janeiro.** Preserved FRUITS and VEGETABLES.

827. **Santos and Ferreirà. Rio de Janeiro.** Nutritive PRESERVES (Conservas alimenticias).
Preserved FRUITS and SWEETS.

828. **Silva Leal and Santos.** PRESERVES.

829. **M. Josè de Castro. Campos, Province of Rio de Janeiro.** Preserved SWEETS.

FLOUR, CRUSHED AND GROUND CEREALS, DECORTICATED GRAINS.

CLASS 557.

830. **Commission for the Province of Sancta Catharina.** Samples of various sorts of FARINA.
FARINA OF MANIOC, prepared from the Fecula of the Manioca Utilissima (Fam. *Euphorbiaceas*), by the process of scraping, pressing and roasting the fecula.
NOTE.—This sort of farina is largely used in Brazil as an alimentary by the population,
FARINA prepared from the orris root, in the Colony of Joinville.
NOTE.—This sort of farina is prepared from the " *Maranta arundinacea*," and is largely used as an excellent alimentary.

831. **Commission for the Province of Pernambuco.** Samples of FARINAS and FECULAS.

832. **Baron de Pirapitinga. Campos. Province of Rio de Janeiro.** PEARLS OF TAPIOCA, prepared in big grains and with the same color of the pearl.

833. **J. Sawerbec. Sancta Catharina.** Samples of ARROW ROOT, ground.

834. **.Factory of Tamancaõ. Province of Maranhão.** Samples of RICE, crushed.

   NOTE —This rice is crushed by hydraulic machines.

835. **M. C. Silva and Filhos. Lage, Province of Rio de Janeiro.** Samples of TAPIOCA.

836. **J. J. Pereira. Province of Sancta Catharina.** FARINA of Manioc. (Bot. *Manioht utilissima.*)

837. **Colony of Angelina. Province of Sancta Catharina.** Samples of WHEAT FLOUR.

838. **M. J. de Lima Carvalho. Province of Sancta Catharina.** Samples of various sorts of FARINA.

839. **Dr. Muricy. Province of Paraná.** Samples of FARINA, prepared from corn and rye.

840. **Dr. J. J. Correa da Silva. Quissaman, Province of Rio de Janeiro.** Samples of FARINA, of MANIOC and TAPIOCA.

841. **Dr. H. R. Alvarenga. Campos, Province of Rio de Janeiro.** FARINACEOUS PRODUCTS.

842. **A. Schemmelpfing. Province of Paraná.** Samples of RYE FLOUR.

843. **Agriculture Fleminensis Institute. Rio de Janeiro.** FARINA or POLVILHO, from Aypim. (Fam. *Euphorbiaceas.*)

   NOTE.—This sort of farina is a healthy nutritive substance, very agreeable to the taste, and also used in the arts.

344. **Commission for the Province of Paraná.** Samples of MANIOC FLOUR and FECULAS.

845. **Commission for the Province of Pernambuco.** Samples of MANIOC and ARROW ROOT FLOURS.

846. **Silvino Tripodi. Province of Paraná.** Samples of crushed RICE.

847. **Dr. Hermelindo de Leão. Province of Paraná.** Samples of crushed RICE.

AGRICULTURAL PRODUCTS. 99

848. **Colony Blumenau, Province of Sancta Catharina.** Samples of Manioc and rice FARINAS.
Samples of ORRIS ROOT.

849. **Colony Blum, Province of Sancta Catharina.** Samples of ORRIS, corn and wheat FLOURS.

850. **Leão and Alves Grist Mill. Province of S. Pedro do Sul.** Samples of wheat FLOUR.

> NOTE.—The exhibitors received rewards at Paris Exhibition (1867), and at all the National Exhibitions for the superior quality of their products.

STARCH AND SIMILAR PRODUCTS.

CLASS 658.

851. **Baron de Pirapitiuga. Campos, Province of Rio de Janeiro.** POLVILHO, or a sort of starch extracted from the Manioht Utilissima.

852. **Commission for the Province of Sancta Catharina.** POLVILHO, extracted from the Manioht Utilissima.

853. **Fleminensis Agriculture Institute. Rio de Janeiro.** Samples of POLVILHO (arrow root).

SUGAR AND SYRUPS.

CLASS 659.

854. **Commission General for the National Exhibition. Rio de Janeiro.** Samples of SUGAR, white, common, and brown, from the Province of Pernambuco.

855. **T. L. de B. Wanderley. Pernambuco.** White SUGAR, filtered.

856. **M. de Souza Leão. Pernambuco.** White SUGAR, filtered.

857. **A. R. Bastos. Pernambuco.** White SUGAR, filtered.

858. **M. B. das Virgens. Pernambuco.** Samples of White SUGAR, filtered.

859. **Franc. P. James Barroso. Campos. Province of Rio de Janeiro.** Samples of SUGAR made from molasses.

860. **Baron da Boa Viagem. Campos. Province of Rio de Janeiro.** Samples of SUGAR made especially for exportation.

861. **Dr. C. T. Pinheiro. Campos. Province of Rio de Janeira.** Samples of SUGAR, prepared with the molasses, and the syrups from sugar cane.

862. **Baron de Villa Franca. Quissamã. Province of Rio de Janeiro.** Samples of White SUGAR.

863. **Paula Vianna. Campos, Province of Rio de Janeiro.** Samples of SUGAR from the sugar cane.

864. **Julião R. de Castro. Campos. Province of Rio de Janeiro.** Samples of SUGAR, prepared with the syrup, from sugar cane.

Samples of SUGAR from honey.

865. **T. B. de Barros. Campos. Province of Rio de Janeiro.** Samples of SUGAR, white and brown.

866. **Mansell, Carré and Co. Rio de Janeiro.** Samples of SUGAR, refined and crystalized.

867. **Affonso M. Dezencourt, Province of Pará.** Samples of crystalized SUGAR.

868. **F. Fernandes de Barros. Province of S. Paulo.** Samples of SUGAR.

869. **Viscount de Mauá. Fazenda da Atalaia, Province of Rio de Janeiro.** Samples of white SUGAR, crystalized.

> NOTE.—This sugar is refined and crystalized without any introductiou of animal carbon in the process. Its price in the market of Rio de Janeiro amounts to 10 cents per pound.

870. **Isidoro Dias. Pernambuco.** Samples of SUGARS and SYRUPS.

871. **Alves de Souza. S. Salvador da Bahia.** Samples of SUGAR.

872. **Costa & Co. Rio de Janeiro.** Samples of refined SUGAR.

873. **Braga & Co. Rio de Janeiro.** SYRUPS.

874. **Presidency of the Province of Bahia.** Samples of refined SUGAR.

WINES, ALCOHOL AND MALT LIQUORS.

CLASS 660.

875. **Commission General for the National Exhibitions. Rio de Janeiro.**
(*a*) SPIRITS and LIQUORS, from the Province of S. Paulo.
(*b*) BRANDY of the best quality, from the Province of Paraná.
(*c*) Matté LIQUOR, from the Province of Paraná.
(*d*) ORANGE WINE, prepared from the juice of the orange, at Assunguy. Province of Paraná.

876. **Commission for the Province of Paraná.** Matté LIQUOR.

877. **Director of the Colony of Jatahy. Rio de Janeiro.** BRANDY, extracted from the sugar-cane.

878. **Braga and Irmão. Rio de Janeiro.** BRANDY, ALCOHOLS and LIQUORS.

879. **D. Vellez Perdigão. Province of Maranhão.** Various DRINKS; VINEGAR extracted from the Pine-apple—white and colored.

880. **Otto Freyung. Sancta Catharina.** Various LIQUORS.

881. **J. L. Guimarães Caipóra. Rio de Janeiro.** LARANGINHA (a sort of orange whisky).

882. **Dr. C. J. Minheiro. Campos, Province of Rio de Janeiro.** LARANGINHA (orange whisky).

883. **Belache. Province of Paraná.** LIQUORS.

884. **Baron da Bella Vista. Bananal, Province of S. Paulo.** BRANDY, from sugar-cane, and orange liquor.

885. **J. do Amaral Rapōso. Pernambuco.** Various LIQUORS.

886. **Dr. J. J. Carneiro da Silva. Macaké, Province of Rio de Janeiro.** LARANGINHA (orange whisky).

AGRICULTURAL PRODUCTS.

887. **M. Roiz. d'Oliveira.** S. Paulo. LIQUORS.

888. **Ignacio J. d'Araujo.** S. Paulo. LIQUORS, WINES and SPIRITS.

889. **Erdmann Cattermolle.** Rio Grande. Province of S. Pedro do Sul. WINES and LIQUORS.

890. **F. Viotti.** Province of Minas Geraes. LIQUOR made from the juice of peaches.

891. **Alves & Co.** Rio de Janeiro. Various LIQUORS.

892. **M. Leitão de Carvalho.** S. Salvadōr da Bahia. GIN, and LARANGINHA (orange whisky).

893. **F. J. Lepage.** Province of Minas Gereas. WINES and VINEGARS.

894. **A. P. C. Mamede.** Province of Ceará. Medicinal WINE of Cajú.

895. **F. L. Correa.** Province of Paraná. WINE of Genipapo, Cajú and orange; BRANDY of sugar-cane.

896. **M. Gil de Macedo.** Sancta Catharina. Various LIQUORS.

897. **F. P. Brandão.** Rio de Janeiro. LIQUORS, WINES, VINEGARS and BRANDY.

898. **J. F. Mattos Pimenta.** Campos. Province of Rio de Janeiro. Hesperidina Saguarembó —SAQUAREMA WINE.

899. **C. Schulman & Co.** Rio de Janeiro. WINE and VINEGAR extracted from the sugar-cane; ALCOHOLIC PREPARATIONS.

900. **Thomaz Geremoabo.** S. Salvadōr da Bahia. AGUARDENTE (brandy) from honey.

901. **E. P. M. Silveira.** Sancta Catharnia, AGUARDENTE (brandy) from sugar-cane.

902. **Braga & Co.** Rio de Janeiro. LARANGINHA AND AGUARDENTE extracted from Aniz; LIQUORS.

903. **F. Lucas Carneiro.** Paraná. VINHO DE PAO (wine of wood.)

904. **Bastos & Camacho.** Paraná. Collection of LIQUORS, viz:— cream of roses, cinnamon, aniz, peppermint, rose and cloves.

AGRICULTURAL PRODUCTS. 103

905. **A. de A. Teixeira. Province of Paraná.** Zestina and Tonic LIQUORS.

906. **J. C. Beloche. Province of Paraná.** LIQUOR of Matté, and GIN.

907. **J. C. Oliveira Filhos. Province of Paraná.** ORANGINA.

908. **Estevaõ J. Pereira. Rio de Janeiro.** LARANGINHA (orange-whisky), AGUARDENTE (brandy), and LOURINHO.

909. **José Boully. Province of Paraná.** WOOD WINE (vinho de pào.)

910. **Commission for Votuverava. Province of Paraná.** WOOD WINE.

911. **J. H. da Silva Rabello. Province of Pará.** LARANGINHA, BRANDY and Cajú WINE.

912. **Paulino P. Falcão. Pernambuco.** BRANDY from sugar-cane.

913. **Baron da Bõa Yiagem. Campos, Province of Rio de Janeiro.** BRANDY distilled from sugar-cane.

914. **Juliáo R. de Castro Filho. Campos, Province of Rio de Janeiro.** BRANDY and spirits distilled from sugar-cane.

915. **Josè R. de Castro. Campos, Province of Rio de Janeiro.** BRANDY distilled from sugar-cane.

916. **Franc. de Paula Gomes Barroso. Campos.** BRANDY and SPIRITS distilled from sugar-cane

917. **J. M. d' Oliveira Vianna. Campos.** BRANDY distilled from sugar-cane.

918. **D. A. G. C. Barrõso. Campos.** ALCOHOL.

919. **J. A. Rapõso. Pernambuco.** WINES and LIQUORS.

920. **Marianno Alves & Co. Rio de Janeiro.** LIQUORS and LARANGINHA (orange whisky.)

921. **M. A. d' Oliveira Pinto. Province of Matto Grosso.** LIQUOR of Cajá, BRANDY distilled from sugar-cane.

922. **M. A. Guimarães. Superagui, Province of Paraná.** WINES.

923. **M. I. M. de Souza. Paranà.** BRANDY distilled from Matté, LARANGINHA (orange whisky.)

Agricultural Products.

924. **J. Olinto Mendes. Province of Paranà.** LIQUOR of Marmello (Guinces.)

925. **Dr. A. J. Macedo. Soares, Province of Paranà.** LIQUOR of Quinces.

926. **B. A, de Menezes. Province of Paranà.** LIQUOR of Quinces.

927. **J. S. C. Castro. Province of Paranà.** LIQUOR of Absynth (worm-wood.)

928. **A. P. Xavier. Province of Paranà.** ALCOHOL of $35°$ distilled from honey, PSEUDO wine of honey, BRANDY distilled also of the honey.

929. **Revd. T. Castelnuovo. Province of Paranà.** Absynth (LIQUOR of worm-wood.)

930. **M. G. de Moraes Rozeira. Campos Geraes, Province of Paranà.** WINES.

931. **Francisco P. de Vasconcellos. Province of Bahia.** ORANGE WINE; ALCOHOLIC DRINKS.

932. **A. M. Carvalho d' Oliveira. Province of Maranhaō.** WINE distilled from sugar-cane, and from various fruits.

933. **Baron d' Itabapoana. Campos, Province of Rio de Janeiro.** LARANGINHA (orange whisky.)

934. **F. M. Celli de Mariz Sarmento. Rio de Janeiro.** LARANGINHA (orange whisky.)

BREAD, BISCUITS, CRACKERS AND CAKES.

CLASS 661.

935. **Dr. Muricy & Ermelindo de Leaō. Province of Paranà.**
BEIJUS of Tapioca, (a sort of biscuit prepared with the farina of Tapioca.

936. **Silva Leal & Santos. Rio de Janeiro.** VERMICELLI.

937. **Commission for the Province of Bahia.** Cakes of CHOCOLATE of musgo.

938. **Franc. do Pinho. Province of Paranà.** Cakes of CHOCOLATE.

VEGETABLE OILS.

CLASS 662.

939. **J. D. Dias.** Province of Amazonas. VEGETABLE OILS.

940. **Eliezer Cohin.** Province of Pará. OIL of Copahiba, (Bot. *Copahifera Miltifuga.*)

942. **Revd. J. B. Cavalcante.** Province of Rio Grande do Nórte. OIL of Andiroba.

943. **J. E. C. Barbósa.** Province of Rio Grande do Nórte. OIL of Batiputà.

944. **J. F. C. Braga.** Province of Alagóas. OIL of Copahiba, superior in quality.

945. **J. A. da Veiga.** Province of Alagóas. OIL of Togo (Bot. *Ilex enropæus.*)

945. **T. R. da Silva.** Province of Alagõas. OIL of Coco, obtained by compression.

946. **M. F. A. Jorge.** Province of Alagõas. OIL of Coco (cocus nocifera)—OIL of Aricuri, (cocus coronata).

947. **A. M. C. Oliveira.** Province of Maranhão. OIL of Tucum (Astrocaryum vulgare).

948. **Frederico Stechel.** Rio de Janeiro. Various OILS.

949. **Barreto Junior.** Province of Parà. OILS of Copahiba, Andiroba and Tucuman-assu.

950. **C. Falcão Dias.** Province of Alagõas. OILS of Batiputà
OILS of Loco (Plumbago scandex.)
OILS of Ricinus (ricinus.)
OILS of Gendiróba (fueillea trilobato.)

951. **R. J. Ferreira Valle.** Alto Mearim. Province of Maranhão.
OIL of the Coco Babassú.

952. **M. L. Vyeira. Province of Maranhão.** OIL of the Coco Babassú.

953. **S. A. Vyeira. Province of Maranhão.** OIL of Andiròba (carapa Guyannensis.)

954. **Commission General for the National Exhibitions. Rio de Janeiro.**
OILS from the Province of Rio Grande do Nórte, namely
OIL of Batiputà (Gomphia parviflora.)
OIL of the Cajù nut.
OIL of Coco.

955. **Commission for the Province of Maranhão.** OIL of Acajà.

956. **Commission for the District of Paulo Affonso. Province of Alagôas.**
OIL of the Cajù nut.

957. **Commission for the Province Ceará.** Various OILS;
OIL of Jurubeba (Solanum Paniculatum, fam. Solanaceous.)
NOTE.—The oil of Jurubeba is esteemed as a powerful specific for the Liver diseases.

958. **The Presidency of the Province of Bahia. S. Salvadōr da Bahia.**
OIL of Ricin (ricinus communis.)
OIL of Coco.

959. **J. Perdigão. Province of Maranhão.** Vegetable OILS.

TEXTILE SUBSTANCES, OF VEGETABLE OR ANIMAL ORIGIN.

COTTON ON THE STEM, IN THE BOLL, GINNED AND BALED.

CLASS 665.

960. **Commission for the Province of Rio Grande do Norte.** (*a*) Samples of cotton, from Ceará Mirim.

> NOTE.—This kind of cotton is taken from a sort of plant called Gossypium herbaceum.

(*b*) Samples of common COTTON.

> NOTE.—This Province, from 1873 to 1874, exported 2,0097,220 kilogr. of cotton, representing the value of nearly 180 thousand dollars.

961. **Commission for the Province of Maranhão.** Samples of COTTON. ginned.

> NOTE.—Cotton is the most important culture of this province; the exportation of this product, from 1873 to 1874, amounted to 3,987,211 kilogr., or the value of 1,150,000 dollars.

962. **Commission for the Province of Pernambuco.** (*a*) Samples of common COTTON and of yellowish COLORED COTTON.

(*b*) Samples of COTTON from the Magdalena factory.

(*c*) Samples of Russian COTTON.

> NOTE.—The cotton from Pernambuco is esteemed for the quality and quantity of the fibre. The cotton tree lasts there for 12 years, and always producing. The exportation of this product from 1873 to 1874 amounted to 12,283,184 kilogr., representing the value of 3 million dollars.

963. **Commission for the Province of Paraná.** Samples of COTTON, baled.

Samples of COTTON, twisted.

964. **Commission for the Municipality of Quebranguelo, Province of Alagoàs.** Samples of COTTON, in the boll, and twisted.

965. Commission for the Province of S. Paulo. Samples of COTTON.

> NOTE.—The culture of cotton in S. Paulo is still made according to the old rules, but its results exceed all calculations. The exportation of this product in the year 1873-1874 amounted to 9,877,482 kilogr,

966. Commission for the Province of Goyaz. Samples of COTTON.

967. Commission for the City of Cuyabá, Province of Matto Grosso. Samples of COTTON.

968. Commission for the Province of Parahyba do Norte. Samples of COTTON on the stem.

> NOTE—This cotton is cultivated at Borborena and Serra Grande, and its price is quoted in the markets the same as that from New Orleans.

> NOTE.—The culture of cotton produces 8 million kilogr. a year, and the exportation amounts to nearly 4,400,000 kilogr.

979. Commission for the Province of Ceará. Samples of COTTON, on the branch.

> NOTE.—This province, from 1873-1874, exported 4,878,044 kilogr. of cotton, or the value of 1,304,324 dollars.

> NOTE.—This cotton is obtained from the plant, *Gossypium arboreum*.

970. Commercial Association Board from Maceió. Province of Alagôas. Samples of COTTON, from "Palmeira dos Indios."

> NOTE.—This cotton is obtained from the plant *Herbaceum Turboreum*.

971. Alexandre C. Moreira. Province of Maranhão. Samples of COTTON on the stem.

> NOTE.—This cotton is considered one of the best in all markets for its whiteness and long fibre, and it takes very well the dye. One kilogramme of bolls produces ½ kil. of cleaned cotton, 73 kilos. of seeds, and 81 litres of oil.

972. M. M. de Miranda. Maceió, Province of Alagôas. Samples of COTTON ginned in wooden cylinders, and preserving intact the fibre.

973. M. E. Souza Athayde. Province of Parana. Samples of COTTON on the stem and with the seed.

974. G. B. T. Rio de Janeiro. Samples of COTTON on the stem.

975. O. J. Soares. Touros, Province of Rio Grande do Norte. Samples of COTTON.

976. Maximilianno Merch. Colony Blumeneau, Province of Sancta Catharina. Samples of COTTON.

977. Eugenia Herbst. Colony Blumenau, Province of Sancta Catharina. Samples of COTTON.

978. D. Rosalina Paes Leme. City of Desterro, Province of Sancta Catharina. Samples of COTTON.

989. Colony Itajahy, Province of Sancta Catharina. Samples of COTTON.

980. F J. Xavier da Silva, Municipe de Castro, Province of Paraná. Samples of COTTON.

981. J. Correia de Mello. Maranguape, Province of Ceará. Samples of COTTON, called *creoulo*.

982. Luiz Maylasky & Co. S. Paulo. Samples of COTTON.

983. Fray Luiz da Grava. S. Salvador da Bahia. Samples of COTTON.

984. Colony of Sancta Maria da Soledade, Province of S. Pedro do Sul. Samples of COTTON.

985. Colony Blumenau, Province of Sancta Catharina. Samples of COTTON.

986. Isaac Decker. Mucury, Province of Minas Geraes. Samples of COTTON.

987. Raymundo J. F. Valle. Province of Maranhão. COTTON on the stem.

988. Martin Hayer. Province of Maranhão. Samples of COTTON on the stem.

999. Commission for Carnaru, Province of Pernambuco. Samples of grey COTTON.

990. L. A. de Sz Barros & Co. Province of S. Paulo. Samples of COTTON.

991. Diogo A. de Barros. Province of S. Paulo. Skeins of COTTON.

992. J. C. A. Limeira, Província of S. Paulo. Samples of COTTON.

993. Dr. J. T. A. C. Constituição, Province of S. Paulo. Samples of COTTON.

HEMPS, FLAX, JUTE, RAMIE, &c., IN PRIMITIVE FORMS AND IN ALL
STAGES OF PREPARATION FOR SPINNING.

CLASS 666.

994. **Commission General for the National Exhibition. Rio de Janeiro.**
HEMP of Imbirussù (Bombax) from the Province of Paraná.
FIBRES of the *Bilbergia tinctoria* from the Province of Paraná.
FIBRES of the Cipó Imbê (*Bot. Philodendron Imbe*) from the Province of S. Paulo.
Collection of FIBRES from the Province of Alagôas.
Various FIBRES from the Province of S. Paulo.

995. **Commission for the Province of Bahia.** PIASSABA (*attalea funifera*).

996. **Commission for the Province of Pernambuco.** Vegetable FIBRES.
NOTE.—Samples of tow, linen of Mairá (*Bactris*), ananaz (*Ananassa sativa*), and Carná Embira (*Xilopia*,)

997. **Commission for the Province of Sancta Catharina.** THREAD of Tucum (*astrocarium tucaman.*)
PAINA, a sort of fibre used for stuffing bolsters, pillows and mattresses.

998. **Commission for Votuveraava. Province of S. Paulo.** ISCA DE ROCEIRA (*Mabea fistuligera*?

999. **Commission for the Province of Parà.** FIBRES from Carrapicho (*Triumfeta semitriloba*).
NOTE.—Largely employed in the industries.
FIBRE of Gravatá (*Bilbergia Tinctoria*).
NOTE.—Largely used in the industries.

1000. **Commission for the Province of Amazonas.** PIASSABA, a sort of Fibre taken from the "attalea funifera" (*Martius*).
FIBRES from the Bertholetia excelsa, largely used for calking vessels.

1001. **L. Gomes de Barros.** **Province of Alagoas.** CIPO MATTA GENTE, used as withes.

1002. **Dr. Muricy.** **Province of Paranà.** CIPO FLORAO (*Malpighiaceas.*)

1003. **Dr. Rego Barros S. Leão.** **Bõa Vista, Province of Pernambuco.** White EMBIRA (*xilopia*).

1004. **Ant J. da Palma.** **Province of Bahia.** Red EMBIRA (*xilopia frutescens*).

1005. **A. F. de Lacerda.** **Province of Bahia.** PIASSABA (*attalea funifera*).

1006. **J. Steele.** **Rio de Janeiro.** Samples of JUTE.

1007. **J. Bley.** **Province of Paranà.** Striga of HEMP (*Linum usitatissimum.*) FIBRES of the Urtica speciosa.

1008. **A. Aguiar de Bãrros.** **Province of S. Paulo.** PAMA (*choriria.*) BARBA DE PAU (*Filandesia*). BRECHA PAULISTANA (*Minordica*).

1009. **M. A. Guimarães.** **Province of Paraná.** BETAS prepared with the barks of the Philodendrom root.

1010. **Rev. P. M. d'Oliveira.** **Province of Amazonas.** TAPURU.
    NOTE.—Largely employed in calking ships.

1011. **Baron da Villa Franca.** **Quissaman, Province of Rio de Janeiro.** PAINA, fine.

1012. **M. Taborda Ribas.** **Province of Paranà.** ISCA of URUPE (*Boltus igniarius*).
    NOTE.—Remarkable also for its medicinal qualities.

1013. **F. Theodóro do Bofim.** **Province of Paranà.** FIBRES of the *Anona silvatica.*

1014. **J. E. Killian.** **Province of Paranà.** FIBRES of the Alves sp. and of the *Urena lobata.*
    NOTE.—Largely used for cordages.

1015. **S.P. Ferreira & J, de S. Negrão.** **Province of Paranà.** FIBRES of the *Cecropia pellata.*
    NOTE.—Used for woven fabrics.

1016. M. A. Guimarães. Province of Paraná. FIBRES of *tucum*.

NOTE.—This sort of fibres is used for cords and fishing lines.

1017. Dr. Agostinho de Leão. Province of Parana. PAINA BARRIGUDA, (*Choriria speciosa*).

NOTE.—Used for stuffing matrasses and pillows.

1018. Flor de Capim. (*Flower of Hail.*)

1019. Severino Leite. Province of Minas Geraes. Samples of various kinds of FIBRES.

NOTE.—Namely:

(1) Cipó lactesceute (*Ascelpiadacea*), which fibre offers a resistance of 100 grammes. The fibre can be extracted two years after the reed has been planted.

(2) Vegetable wool from the leaves of the Palma tree, "Iriuba" or Brajaúba. (Medium of resistance 41 grammes.)

(3) Cipo vermelho (*Malpighiacea*) obtained from the bark of the reed and with the peculiarity that it takes a red dye when extracted. (Medium of resistance 49 grammes.)

(4) Cipó preto (*Malpighiacea*), so called because the fibre takes a black dye during the process of separation. (Medium of resistance 36 grammes.

(5) Paper or leaves of the fig tree (*Ficus speciosus*) furnishing very good writing paper.

1020. B. A. da Cruz & Florindo T. do Bomfin. Province of Paranà. FIBRES of the *Copaifera officinalis*.

FIBRES of Bombax.

1021. Felix F. Portella. Rio Bonito, Province of Pernambuco. FIBRES of *Gravata assu*.

Samples of VEGETABLE HAIR, white and coloured.

NOTE.—These vegetable hairs are used for stuffing matrasses.

1022. Gaspar P. Ferreira & Comp. Province of Paraná. FIBRES of the Umbauba tree (*Cecropia.*)

1023. **F. Theodóre do Bomfin and others. Province of Paraná.** FIBRES of araticum ipè (*anona sylvatica*).
FIBRES of Imbivurrû (*Bombax.*)
FIBRES of copaiba (*Copaifera.*)

1024. **D. Rosalina Paes Leme. Desterro. Province of Sancta Catharina.** Samples of FLAX.

1025. **Phillippe Keller. S. João de Montenegro. Province of S. Pedro do Sul.** Samples of FLAX.

1026. **Baron de Kalden. Cachoeira. Province of S. Pedro do Sul.** FLAX.

1027. **Carlos Ackermann and G. Bladern. New Petropolis. Province of S. Pedro do Sul.** FLAX, prepared.

1028. **F. Fernandes de Barros. Province of S. Paulo.** FIBRES of Tucum.

1029. **Dr. E. de Leão. Province of Parana.** FLAX.

1030. **A. Rufino d'Almeida. Perna.mbuco**
   (*a*) FIBRE from the *Triumphetta semitriloba*, largely used in the industry.
   (*b*) FIBRES from the *Bertholetia Excelsa*, largely used for calking ships.
   (*c*) FIBRES of the *Xilopia Sericea.*
   NOTE.---The *Xilopia sericea* produces fibres, wide and very long, and which are highly esteemed in mechanical industries and for various fabrics.

1031. **Commission for the Province of Ceará.**
   (*a*) Fibres of Tucum, (*Astrocarium tucuman*).
   NOTE.—Largely used in mechanical industry.
   (*b*) PAINA of Gravata (*Bilbergia*).
   NOTE.—Used in the industry and for stuffing pillows and matresses.

1032. **Lang & Co. Province of Paraná.** Samples of HEMP and FLAX.

WOOL IN THE FLEECE, CARDED AND IN BALES.

CLASS 667.

1033. **Instituto Fluminense d' Agricultura. Rio de Janeiro.** Samples of Wool.

1034. **A. Schimmelpfing. Province of Paranà.** Samples of white and black Wool.

1035. **Ernesto Wirmond. Province of Paranà.** Wool of the sheep called *Negresto merino*.

1036. **Commission for the Province of Paranà.** Samples of Wool.

1037. **Commission for the Province of Alagoãs.** Samples of vegetable Wool.

SILK IN THE COCOON AND REELED.

CLASS 668.

1038. **Luiz Ribeiro de Souza Rezende. Itaguahy. Rio de Janeiro.** Cocoons formed by the silk worm, and samples of silk reeled. Culture of the Bombix.
   Note.—The Seropedic establishment of Mr. Luiz de Rezende is a large one, and occupies an area of 800 thousand square fathoms. The number of Mulberry-trees growing there amounts to 60 thousand, and he is able to cultivate from 30 to 40 ounces of silk worms, producing 24 to 30 thousand pounds of silk.

1039. **Pedro A. dos Santos Reis & Co. Rio Grande. Province of S. Pedro do Sul.** Samples of Silk, reeled.
   Note.—This silk is of a superior quality and obtained from the *Bombix mori*. Each cocoon contains nearly 3,600 metres of silk thread, of which 600 metres can be utilized.

1040. Franc de Paula Mello Netto. **Province of Minas Geraes.** Cocoons of the SILK WORM,

1041. Paulo Schrazer. **Colony Blumenau. Province of Sancta Catharina.** COCOONS of the silk worm.

1042. Eugenia & T. **Province of Minas Geraes.** Samples of white SILK.

1043. Dr. Nicolau J. Moreira. **Rio de Janeiro.** SILKS in the cocoon and Butter-fly " Porta Espelhos." (See class 638.)

HAIR, BRISTLES.

CLASS 669.

1044. **Commission General for the National Exhibitions. Rio de Janeiro.** HAIRS and HORSE-HAIRS, from the Province of Paraná.

1045. **Commission for the Province of Pernambuco.** BRISTLES.

1046. **Commission for the Province of Paraná.** Samples of HAIR.

MACHINES, IMPLEMENTS AND PROCESSES OF MANUFACTURE.

TILLAGE.

CLASS 670.

1047. Bierrenback & Irmão. **Campinas. Province of S. Paulo.** Four PLOWS.

1048. J. Blanchet. **Province of Paraná.** Small PLOWS.

1049. **Commission for the Province of S. Paulo.** PLOWS.

1050. **Commission for the Province of Paraná.** PLOW.

COMMERCIAL FERTILIZERS.

CLASS 681.

1051. **Commission for the Province of Amazonas.** GUANO.

1052. **Drs. Muricy & Leão.** Province of Paraná. GUANO.

WOMEN'S DEPARTMENT.

A. A.—Artificial Flowers.
B. B. B.—Embroideries and Tapestry.
C. C. C.—Laces, Sieves and Crochets.

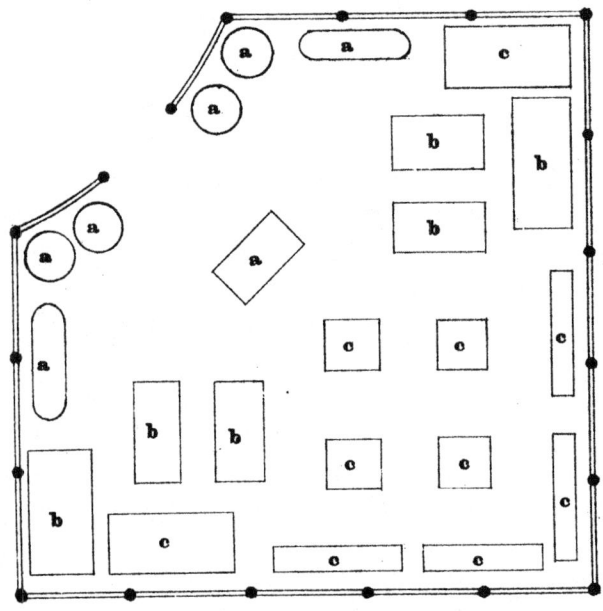

Women's Pavilion

Scale ⅛ Inch = one foot.

WOMEN'S DEPARTMENT.

EMBROIDERIES, LACES, SIEVES, Etc.

EMBROIDERIES.

CLASS 252.

1053. **The orphan girls of the School of the Imperial Society, "Amante de Instrucção, Rio de Janeiro.** EMBROIDERIES of golden thread on velvet.

CUSHION covered with embroidery work.

1054. **The Girls of the Immacculate Conception School. Ceará.** STOLE for Priest, embroidered.

1055. **Baroness of Itamarati. Rio de Janeiro.** PIN CUSHION, embroidered on satin.

WATCH-HOLDER, embroidered with golden thread on silk.

1056. **Miss Capitolina A. d'Araujo. Rio de Janeiro.** WATCH-HOLDER, embroidered and imitating the shape of a slipper.

1057. **The Orphans of the Sancta Thereza School. Rio de Janeiro.** STOLE for Priest, embroidery work of golden thread on silk.

CUSHION covered wiih a piece of embroidery, made with golden and silk threads on velvet.

1058. **Mrs. Maria Pinto Netto. Campos, Province of Rio de Janeiro.** ROBE DE CHAMBRE, embroidered.

TOWELS, bordered with embroideries on linen.

WOMEN'S DEPARTMENT.

1059. Miss N. A. C. Cunha. S. Salvador de Bahia. CUSHION, covered with a piece of embroidery made of golden and silk threads on silk.

1060. Miss D. A. Julia Dias. Maceió, Province of Alagoas. CUSHION, covered with embroidery work.

1061. M. Antonio Chaves. Embroidery School for Women. Rio de Janeiro. CUSHION, covered with embroidery work.

1062. Baroness de Pirapitinga. Campos, Province of Rio de Janeiro. TOWEL, enriched with embroidery on linen and lace bordered.

1663. Baroness da Boa Viagem. Campos, Province of Rio de Janelro. TOWELS and PILLOW-SHAMS, enriched with embroideries on linen.

LACES, SIEVES AND CROCHETS.

1064. Mrs. Maria Pinte. Netto-Campos. UNDER-SKIRT, lace-bordered. Crochet work, in relief.

1065. Baroness de Piraptinga. Campos. TOWELS and PILLOW SHAM, sieve and lace bordered.

1066. Baroness do Bõa Viagem. Campos. TOWELS, lace bordered.

1067. Mrs. Eulalia de Saldanha da Gama. (Rio de Janeiro. TOWEL and PILLOW SHAM, enriched with labyrinth lace ; both presented to her Imperial Highness the Princess D. Isabel.

1068. Her Imperial Highness the Princess D. Isabel. Rio de Janeiro. Pair of PILLOW SHAMS, enriched with labyrinth lace.

1069. Miss Maria Thereza d'Oliveira Vianna. Campos. COVERLID, Crochet work made with woolen thread.

1070. Baroness de Suruhy, Rio de Janeiro. COVERLID, crochet work.

1071. The Girls of the Municipal School of S. José. Rio de Janeiro. COVERLIDS for chairs, made of crochet.

1071. **Mrs. Augusta de Barros Pimentel.** **Province of Alagôas.** Lace TIE for lady's garments, handkerchiefs, sieve and lace bordered, all made by Miss Emilia de Paiva.

1072. **Mrs. Roza Callado.** A piece of labyrinth LACE for lady's garments.

1073. **Commission for the Province of Ceará.** **Fortaleza.** HANDKERCHIEFS and TOWELS, cut in sieve and lace bordered, by the women of the Province.

1074. **Commission for the Province of Rio Grande do Nórte.** **Natal.** HANDKERCHIEFS, TOWELS, LACES and PILLOW SHAMS, enriched with sieve and laces made by the women of the Province.

1075. **Commission for the Province of Parahyba do Nórte.** **Parahyba.** HANDKERCHIEFS, TOWELS, LACES and PILLOW SHAMS, enriched with lace and seive, made by the women of the Province.

1076. **Commission for the Povince of Alagöas.** **Maceió.** HANDKERCHIEFS, LACES and PILLOW SHAMS, enriched with lace and seive, made by the women of the Province.

1077. **D. Umbelina J. da Cósta.** **Icó, Province of Ceará.** TOWEL, cut in labyrinth lace.

1078. **The Orphan Girls of the Immaculate Conception School.** **Ceará.** TOWEL, cut in sieve and labyrinth lace with small squares, each square with a design, and executed by a different girl.

1079. **Mrs. Zulmira Cintra da Silva.** **Rio de Janeiro.** ROBE DE FRIVOLITE, for child.

TAPESTRY AND FANCY WORKS.

1080. **The Girl Leonōr T. Barros, Rio de Janeiro.** Work of tapestry representing the "HOLY MOTHER."

1081. **Idelvira Fluminense (girl 10 years old,) Rio de Janeiro.** Work of TAPESTRY.

WOMEN'S DEPARTMENT.

1082. Isabel S. das Neves, (girl of the Municipal School of S. Sebastiaô,) Rio de Janeiro. A pair of CUSHIONS covered with tapestry work

1083. Alzira A. d'Oliveira (girl of the Municipal School of S. Joseph,) Rio de Janeiro. CUSHION covered with tapestry work.

1084. The Orphan Girls of the Santa Thereza School, Rio de Janeiro. CUSHIONS covered with tapestry work.

1085. The Girls of the Immaculate Conception School, Ceará. CUSHIONS covered with tapestry work.

1086. The Orphan Girls of the Misèricord School. CUSHION covered with tapestry work.

1087. C. Augusta da Matta (girl of the Municipal School of S. Sebastiaô,) CUSHION covered with tapestry work.

1088. Henriquèta M. Neves (girl of the Municipal School of S. Josè,) Rio de Janeiro. CUSHION covered with tapestry work.

1089. Maria da Glória Martins (girls of the Municipal School of S. Sebastian,) Rio de Janeiro. TAPESTRY WORK.

1090. Miss Maria D. Pègo de Faria (School of Sancta Cecilia, Rio de Janeiro. CUSHION.

1091. Miss Capitolina A. d'Araujo, Rio de Janeiro. FRAME made of paste board, cut with a penknife and containing a portrait of His Majesty the Emperor of Brazil.

1092. Miss Paulina M. de Barros, Rio de Janeiro. LETTER KEEPER made of paste board, and cut with a pen knife.
PIN-BOX, made of paste board, and cut with a pen-knife.

1093. Miss Anna M. Serzedello de Faria. Pará. FRAME representing a castle made of cork and cut with a pen-knife.

1094. H. J. Linhares. S. Francisco. Pair of BOOTS, made of tapestry work.

1095. Mrs. Joanna Honaldi. Rio de Janeiro. NEEDLE-WORK representing the portrait of His Majesty the Emperor of Brazil.

ARTIFICIAL FLOWERS.

CLASS 254.

1096. **Misses Natte. Rio de Janeiro.** FLOWERS, COIFFURES and all sorts of garments made of feathers, and remarkable for their natural colours, rare choice and good taste.

1097. **Misses Silveira de Souza. Destèrro, Province of Sancta Catharina.** Boquet of ARTIFICIAL FLOWERS made of fish scale, egg skin, shells, wood and feathers.

> NOTE.—The fish scale flowers are most worthy of attention for their delicate perfection, and novelty of workmanship.

1098. **The Orphan Girls of the Immaculate Conception School. Ceará.** BOUQUET of feather flowers.

1099. **Mrs. Rosalinda Paes Leme. Sancta Catharina.** BOUQUET of leather flowers.

1100. **A. Guimarães. Paraná.** BOUQUET of fish scale flowers.

1101. **The Nuns of the Convent of Merces. S. Paulo.** FLOWER. cut with pen-knife in the fig tree rim.

1102. **Her Imperial Highness the Princess D. Isabel. Rio de Janeiro.** CROWN OF FLOWERS, made with cereals.

1103. **Commission for the Province of Bahia.** BOUQUET of feather flowers, made by different women.

1104. **Miss Emilia L. dos Santos Pōrto. Rio de Janeirō.** FLOWER-STAND made of leather.

CLASSIFICATION

AND

GROUPINGS OF EXHIBITS,

AS ARRANGED BY THE

United States Centennial Commission,

FOR THE

INTERNATIONAL EXHIBITION 1876

AT

PHILADELPHIA.

GROUP I.

MINERALS, MINING AND METALLURGY, INCLUDING THE MACHINERY.

Class 100.—Minerals, Ores, etc.

Metallic and non-metallic minerals, exclusive of coal and oil. Collections of materials systematically arranged; collections of ores and associated minerals; geological collections.

Class 101.—Mineral Combustibles.

Coal—anthracite, semi-bituminous, and bituminous—coal-waste and pressed coal; albertite, asphalt, and asphaltic limestone; bitumen, mineral tar, crude petroleum.

Class 102.—Building Stones, Marble, Slates, etc.

Rough, hewn, sawed, or polished, for buildings, bridges, walls, or other constructions, or for interior decoration, or for furniture.

Marble—white, black, or colored—used in building, decoration, statuary, monuments, or furniture, in blocks or slabs not manufactured.

Class 103.

Cement-stone and crude materials for cement, limestone, etc. (For cement and artificial stone, see Group II.)

Class 104.

Clays, kaolin, silex, and other materials for the manufacture of bricks, terra-cotta, porcelain, faience, and of glass, tiles, and firebrick. Refractory stones for lining furnaces, sand-stone, steatite, etc., and refractory furnace materials.

Class 105.

Graphite—crude and refined—for polishing purposes; for lubricating, electrotyping, photography, pencils, etc.

Class 106.

Grindstones, hones, whetstones, grinding and polishing materials—sand quartz, garnet, crude topaz, diamond, corundum, emery in the rock and pulverized, and in assorted sizes, and grades; lithographic stones.

Class 107.

Mineral waters; artesian well water; natural brines; salt; soluble minerals generally; sulphur, etc.

Class 108.

Mineral fertilizing substances—gypsum, phosphate of lime, marls, shells, coprolites, etc., not manufactured.

METALS, METALLURGICAL PRODUCTS, AND PROCESSES.

Class 110.

Gold, silver, platinum, quicksilver, iridium and the rare metals.

Class 111.

Iron and steel in the pig, ingot, bar, plates and sheets; with specimens of slags, fluxes, residues, and products of working.

Class 112.

Copper in ingots, bars, and rolled, with specimens illustrating its various stages of production.

Class 113.

Lead, zinc, antimony, and other metals, the result of extractive processes.

Class 114.

Alloys used as materials—brass, nickel-silver, solder, etc.

Class 115.

Electro-metallurgy—unwrought products.

MACHINES, TOOLS, AND APPARATUS [OF MINING, AND METALLURGY.

Class 500.

Rock drilling, boring and cutting.

Class 501.

Well and shaft boring, oil-well machinery, etc.

Class 502.

Machines, apparatus, and implements for coal cutting.

Class 503.

Hoisting machinery and accessories.

Class 504.

Pumping, draining, and ventilating.

Class 505.

Crushing, grinding, sorting, and dressing—breakers, stamps, mills, pans, screens, sieves, jigs, concentrators.

Class 506.

Furnaces, smelting apparatus, and accessories.

CLASS 507.

Machinery used in the Bessemer and other special processes for making steel.

CLASS 512.

Rolling mills, bloom squeezers, etc.

MINE ENGINEERING—MODELS, MAPS AND SECTIONS.

CLASS 120.

Surface and underground surveying and plotting. Projection of underground work, location of shafts, tunnels, etc. Surveys for aqueducts, and drainage.

Boring and drilling rocks, shafts, and tunnels, etc., and for ascertaining the nature and extent of mineral deposits.

Construction. Sinking and lining shafts by various methods, driving and timbering tunnels, and generally the operations of opening, stoping and breaking down ore; timbering, lagging and masonry.

Hoisting and delivering at the surface, rock, ore, or miners.

Pumping and draining by engines, buckets, or by adits.

Ventilation and lighting.

Subaqueous mining, blasting, etc.

Hydraulic mining, and the various processes and methods of sluicing and washing auriferous gravel, and other superficial deposits.

Quarrying.

CLASS 121.

Models of mines, of veins, and of machinery, etc.

GROUP II.

POTTERY, GLASS, ARTIFICIAL STONES, ETC.

Class 206.

Bricks, drain-tiles, terra-cotta, and architectural pottery.

Class 207.

Fire-clay goods, crucibles, pots, furnaces, bricks and slabs.

Class 208.

Tiles—plain, enameled, encaustic; geometric tiles and mosaics. Tiles for pavements and for roofing, etc.

Class 209.

Porcelain for purposes of construction—hardware, trimmings, etc.

Class 210.

Stone china, for household use, for chemists, druggists, etc.; earthenware, stone-ware, faience, etc.

Class 211.

Majolica and Palissy ware.

Class 212.

Biscuitware, Parian, etc.

Class 213.

Porcelain ware for table and toilet use, and for decoration.

Class 214.

Glass used in construction and for mirrors. Window glass of various grades of quality and of size. Plate glass—rough, and ground or polished. "Toughened glass."

Class 215.

Chemical and pharmaceutical glass-ware, vials, bottles.

Class 216.

Table glass and movable decorative glassware.

Class 219.

Stained and enameled glass, cut and engraved window glass, signs, lanterns and similar decorative objects.

Class 103.

Lime cement, and hydraulic cement raw and burned, accompanied by specimens of the crude rock or material used, also artificial stone, concrete, beton.

Specimens of lime mortar and mixtures, with illustrations of the process of mixing, etc.

Beton mixtures and results, with illustrations of the processes.

Artificial stone for building purposes, building blocks, cornices, etc.

Artificial stone mixtures, for pavements, walls, or ceilings.

Plasters, mastics, etc.

Class 517.

Brick, pottery and tile machines. Machines for making artificial stone.

Class 518.

Furnaces, moulds, blow-pipes, etc., for making glass and glass-ware.

GROUP III.

CHEMISTRY AND PHARMACY, INCLUDING THE APPARATUS.

CLASS 200.—CHEMICALS, PHARMACEUTICAL PREPARATIONS, ETC.

Mineral acids, and the methods of manufacture. Sulphuric, nitric, and hydrochloric acids.

The common commercial alkalies—potash, soda, and ammonia, with their carbonates.

Salt and its production. Salt manufactured from deposits—native salt. Salt by solar evaporation from sea-water. Salt by evaporation from water or saline springs or wells. Rock salt. Ground and table salt.

Bleaching powders, chloride of lime, etc.

Chemicals and chemical compounds generally.

Pharmaceutical compounds.

CLASS 274.

Pharmaceutical apparatus.

CLASS 201.—OILS, SOAPS, CANDLES, ILLUMINATING GASES, ETC.

Oils from mineral, animal, and vegetable sources. Refined petroleum, benzine, naptha, and other products of the manufacture. Oils from various seeds, refined, and of various degrees of purity, such as olive oil, cotton seed oil, palm oil. Animal oils, of various kinds, in their refined state. Oils prepared for special purposes besides lighting and for food. Lubricating oils.

Soaps and detergent preparations.

Candles—stearine, glycerine, paraffine, etc.; spermaceti.

Illuminating gas and its manufacture.

Oxygen gas, and its applications for heating, lighting, metallurgy, and as a remedial agent.

Chlorine and carbonic acid.

Class 202.

Paints, pigments, dyes, colors, turpentine, varnishes, printing inks, writing inks, blacking.

Class 203.

Flavoring extracts, essences, perfumery, pomades, cosmetics.

Class 659.

Sugar, syrups, and sugar making apparatus.

Class 508.

Chemical manufacturing machinery.

Class 509.

Gas machinery and apparatus.

GROUP IV.

ANIMAL AND VEGETABLE PRODUCTS, AND THE MACHINERY FOR THEIR PREPARATION.

CLASS 650.

Sponges, sea-weed, and other growths used for food or in the arts.

CLASS 651.

The Dairy—milk, cream, butter, cheese.

CLASS 652.

Tallow, oil, and lard ; ivory, bone, horn, glue.

CLASS 653.

Eggs, feathers, down.

CLASS 654.

Honey and wax.

CLASS 655.

Animal perfumes—as musk, civet, ambergris, etc.

CLASS 656.

Preserved meats, vegetables, and fruit ; dried, or in cans or jars. Meat and vegetable extracts.

CLASS 657.

Flour—crushed and ground cereals ; decorticated grains.

Class 658.

Starch and similar products.

(For sugar, syrups, etc., see Group 111.)

Class 660.

Wines, alcohol, and malt liquors.

Class 661.

Bread, biscuits, crackers, and cakes.
(For vegetable and other oils, see Group 111.)
Yeast preparations, yeast powders, baking powders, etc.

GROUP V.

FISH AND FISH PRODUCTS—APPARATUS OF FISHING, ETC.

Class 640.

Marine mammals—seals, cetaceans, etc., specimens living in aquaria, or stuffed, salted, or otherwise preserved.

Class 641.

Fishes, living or preserved.

Class 642.

Pickled fish, and parts of fish used for food.

Class 643.

Crustaceans, echinoderms, beche-de-mer.

Class 644.

Mollusks, oysters, clams, etc., used for food.

Class 645.

Shells, corals, and pearls.

Class 646.

Whalebone, shagreen, fish-glue, isinglass, sounds.

Class 647.

Instruments and apparatus of fishing—nets, baskets, hooks, and other apparatus used in catching fish.

Class 648.

Fish culture—aquaria, hatching pools, vessels for transporting roe and spawn, and other apparatus used in fish breeding, culture or preservation.

GROUP VI.

TIMBER, WORKED LUMBER, PARTS OF BUILDINGS, FORESTRY.

CLASS 600.

Timber and trunks of trees, entire or in transverse or truncated sections, with specimens of barks, leaves, flowers, seed vessels, and seed.

Ship timber—masts, spars, knees; longitudinal sections of trees; railway ties, planks, boards, rough and planed; shingles, laths, staves, etc.

Timber and lumber prepared in various ways to resist decay and combustion, as by injection of salts of copper and zinc, etc.

CLASS 601.

Ornamental woods used in decorating and for furniture, such as mahogany, oak, etc., and veneers of rosewood, ebony, walnut, maple, madrona and other woods.

CLASS 602.

Dye-woods, barks, and galls for coloring and tanning. (See also Group III.)

CLASS 603.

Gums, resins, caoutchouc, gutta percha, vegetable wax.

Lichens, mosses, fungi, pulu, ferns.

CLASS 605.

Seeds, nuts, etc., for food and ornamental purposes.

Class 604.

Class 606.

Forestry—illustrations of the art of planting, managing, and protecting forests. Statistics.

Class 227.

Manufactured parts of buildings—doors, mouldings, sash, blinds, mantels, etc.

Parquetry work, detached specimens for floors, wainscoting, etc. (For complete designs, etc., see Group XXVII.)

GROUP VII.

FURNITURE, UPHOLSTERY, WOODEN WARE, BASKETS, Etc.

Class 217.

Household, office, and church furniture.

Upholstery, curtain fixtures, shades, etc.

Class 220.

Mirrors, guilt cornices, brackets, picture frames, etc.

Class 221.

The nursery and its accessories—children's chairs, walking chairs.

Class 289.

Wooden and basket ware, papier maché.

Class 286.

Brushes, brooms, dusters, etc.

Class 225.

Laundry appliances—washing-machines, mangles, clothes-wringers, clothes-bars, ironing-tables.

Class 226.

Apparatus and appliances of the bath room and water-closet—shower bath, earth closet, etc.

Class 290.

Undertakers' furnishing goods—caskets, coffins, etc.

GROUP VIII.

COTTON, LINEN, AND OTHER FABRICS, INCLUDING THE MATERIALS AND THE MACHINERY.

CLASS 228.—WOVEN FABRICS OF MINERAL ORIGIN.

Wire cloths, sieve cloths, wire screens, bolting cloths, Asbestos fibre, spun and woven, with the clothing manufactured from it. Glass thread, floss and fabrics.

CLASS 229.

Coarse fabrics, of grass, rattan, cocoanut, and bark.

Mattings—Chinese, Japanese, palm-leaf, grass and rushes. Floor cloths of rattan and cocoanut fibre, aloe fibre, etc.

CLASS 665.

Cotton on the stem, in the boll, ginned, and baled.

CLASS 666.

Hemp, flax, jute, ramie, etc., in primitive forms and in all stages of preparation for spinning.

CLASS 230.

Cotton yarns and fabrics, bleached and unbleached. Cotton sheeting and shirting, plain and twilled.

Cotton canvas and duck. Awnings, tents.

CLASS 231.

Dyed cotton fabrics, exclusive of prints and calicoes.

Class 232.

Cotton prints and calicoes, including handkerchiefs, scarfs, etc.

Class 233.

Linen and other vegetable fabrics, uncolored or dyed.

Class 234.

Floor oil cloths, and other painted and enameled tissues, and imitations of leather with a woven base.

Class 521.

Machines for the manufacture of cotton goods.

Class 523.

Machines for the manufacture of linen goods.

Class 524.

Machines for the manufacture of rope and twine, and other fibrous materials not elsewhere specified.

GROUP IX.

WOOL AND SILK FABRICS, INCLUDING THE MATERIALS AND THE MACHINERY.

WOVEN AND FELTED GOODS OF WOOL, AND MIXTURES OF WOOL.

CLASS 667.

Wool in the fleece, in bales, and corded.

CLASS 235.

Card wool fabrics—yarns, broadcloth, doeskins, fancy cassimeres. Felted goods. Hat bodies.

CLASS 236.

Flannels—plain flannels, domets, opera and fancy.

CLASS 237.

Blankets, robes, and shawls.

CLASS 238.

Combed wool fabrics—worsteds, yarns, dress goods for women's wear, delaines, serges, poplins, merinoes.

CLASS 239.

Carpets, rugs, etc.—Brussels, melton, tapestry, tapestry Brussels, Axminster, Venitian, ingrain, felted carpetings, druggets, rugs, etc.

CLASSIFICATION. 21

CLASS 240.

Hair—alpaca, goat's hair, camel's hair, and other fabrics mixed or unmixed with wool.

CLASS 241.

Printed and embossed woolen cloths, table covers, patent velvets.

CLASS 522.

Machines for the manufacture of woolen goods.

SILK AND SILK FABRICS, AND MIXTURES IN WHICH SILK IS THE PREDOMINATING MATERIAL.

CLASS 242.

Cocoons and raw silk as reeled from the cocoon; thrown or twisted silks in the gum.

CLASS 243.

Thrown or twisted silks, boiled off or dyed; in hanks, skeins or on spools.

CLASS 244.

Spun silk yarns and fabrics, and the materials from which they are made.

CLASS 245.

Plain woven silks, lutestrings, sarsnets, satins, serges, foulards, tissues for hat and millinery purposes, etc.

CLASS 246.

Figured silk piece goods, woven or printed. Upholstery silks, etc.

Class 247.

Crapes, velvets, gauzes, cravats, handkerchiefs, hoisery, knit goods, laces, scarfs, ties, veils, all descriptions of cut and made up silks.

Class 248.

Ribbons—plain, fancy, and velvet.

Class 249.

Bindings—braids, cords, galloons, ladies' dress trimmings, upholsters', tailors', military, and miscellaneous trimmings.

Class 520.

Machines for the manufacture of silk goods.

GROUP X.

CLOTHING, FURS, INDIA RUBBER GOODS, ORNAMENTS, AND FANCY ARTICLES.

(Exclusive of leather boots and shoes.)

CLASS 250.

Ready-made clothing, knit goods and hoisery, military clothing, church vestments, costumes, water-proof clothing and clothing for special objects.

CLASS 251.

Hats, caps, gloves, mittens, etc.; straw and palm leaf hats; bonnets, and millinery.

CLASS 252.

Laces, embroideries, and trimmings for clothing, furniture, and carriages.

CLASS 254.

Artificial flowers, coiffures, buttons, trimmings, pins, hooks-and-eyes, fans, umbrellas, sun-shades, walking-canes, pipes, and small objects of dress or adornment, exclusive of jewelry.

Toys, games, etc.

CLASS 255.

Fancy leather work—pocket-books, toilet cases, traveling equipments, valises and trunks. (See also in Leather, Group XII.)

CLASS 257.

Furs manufactured into clothing, robes, etc.

CLASS 258.

Historical collection of costumes; national costumes.

CLASS 288.

Flags, insignia, emblems.

CAOUTCHOUC AND GUTTA PERCHA INDUSTRY.

CLASS 285.

"India rubber" goods and manufactures.

GROUP XI.

JEWELRY, WATCHES, SILVER-WARE, BRONZES, Etc.

(*See also Group* XXVII ART.)

CLASS 253.

Jewelry, and ornaments worn upon the person.

Diamonds, and other precious gems, mounted singly or in groups—head-dresses, "tiara," necklaces, rings, pins, etc.

Pearls, pearl and coral sets and ornaments.

Gold ornaments—rings, pins, necklaces, chains, bracelets, buttons, etc.

Cut and engraved stones.

Gilt goods, metal and other ornaments, and imitations generally.

Watches—their mounting and decoration—regarded chiefly from the ornamental and commercial point of view. For "movements" and chronometric qualities, see also Group XXV.

Silver-ware and silver-plate—hollow-ware, plain, embossed, engraved, or otherwise ornamented.

Silver and silver plated knives, forks, spoons, etc.

Ornamental silver bronze and metal work generally. Bronzes and "mantel ornaments," decorative clocks, etc. Enamels, etc. (See Group XXVII.)

GROUP XII.

LEATHER AND MANUFACTURES OF LEATHER, INCLUDING BOOTS, SHOES, TRUNKS, Etc.

(*For Harness and Saddlery, in part, see Group* XVII.)

Hides and skins, salted or dried.
Leather of all kinds.
Parchment, vellum, etc.
Boots and shoes.
Trunks, and traveling equipments, in part.
Belting, cords, straps, etc.
Harness and saddlery. (See Group XVII.)

Class 532.

Machines for preparing and working leather.

Class 533.

Machines for making boots and shoes.

GROUP XIII.

PAPER INDUSTRY, STATIONERY, PRINTING, AND BOOK MAKING.

Class 258.

Stationery for the desk, stationers' articles, pens, pencils, inkstands, and other apparatus of writing and drawing.

Class 259.

Writing paper and envelopes, blank-book paper, bond paper, tracing paper, drawing paper, tracing linen, tissue paper, etc.

Class 260.

Printing papers; for books, newspapers, etc.

Wrapping paper of all grades; cartridge and manilla paper, paper bags.

Class 261.

Blank books, sets of account books, specimens of ruling and binding, including blanks, bill heads, etc.; book binding.

Class 262.

Cards—playing cards, card board, binders' board, pasteboard, paper or card board boxes.

Class 263.

Building paper, pasteboard for walls, cane fibre felt, papier maché, and materials for construction, car wheels, ornaments, etc.

Class 264.

Wall papers, enameled and colored papers, imitations of leather, wood, etc.

MACHINES AND APPARATUS FOR TYPE SETTING, PRINTING, STAMPING, EMBOSSING, AND FOR MAKING BOOKS AND PAPER WORKING.

Class 540.

Printing presses.

Class 541.

Type-casting machines, apparatus of stereotyping.

Class 542.

Types and type-setting machines. Type-writing machines.

Class 543.

Printers' furniture.

Class 544.

Book-binding machines.

Class 545.

Paper-folding machines.

Class 546.

Paper and card cutting machines.

Class 547.

Envelope machines.

Class 525.

Paper making machinery and process.

GROUP XIV.

APPARATUS FOR HEATING, LIGHTING, VENTILATION, WATER SUPPLY, AND DRAINAGE.

CLASS 222.

Apparatus and fixtures for heating and cooking—stoves, ranges, heaters, etc.

Fire places, grates and fixtures, for burning wood, coal or gas.

Hot air furnaces, steam heaters, hot water heaters, radiators, etc.

Stoves, cooking stoves, kitchen ranges, ovens, and fixed apparatus of cooking.

CLASS 224.

Kitchen and pantry utensils, tin-ware, and apparatus used in cooking (exclusive of cutlery).

CLASS 223.

Apparatus for lighting—gas fixtures, lamps, etc.

Ventilating apparatus.

Water supply apparatus—pipes, faucets, filters, hot-water boilers, water-backs and plumbers' goods generally.

Drainage—Pipes, traps, and sewer connections, and apparatus.

GROUP XV.

BUILDER'S HARDWARE, EDGE TOOLS, CUTLERY, Etc.

Class 280.

Hand tools and instruments used by carpenters, joiners, and for wood and stone in general. Miscellaneous hand tools used in industries, such as jewelers, engravers.

Class 281.

Cutlery—knives, penknives, scissors, razors, razor-strops, skates, and implements sold by cutlers.

Class 283.

Metal hollow-ware—ornamental castings.

Class 284.

Hardware used in construction, exclusive of tools and implements, spikes, nails, screws, tacks, bolts, locks, latches, hinges, pulleys. Furniture fittings; ship's hardware. (For carriage hardware, see Group XVII.)

GROUP XVI.

MILITARY AND SPORTING ARMS, WEAPONS, APPARATUS OF HUNTING, EXPLOSIVES, Etc.

Class 265.

Military small-arms, muskets, pistols, and magazine guns, with their ammunition.

Class 266.

Light artillery, compound guns, machine guns, mitrailleuses, etc.

Class 267.

Heavy ordnance and its accessories.

Class 268.

Knives, swords, spears, and dirks.

Class 269.

Fire arms used for sporting and hunting, also other implements for the same purpose.

Class 270.

Traps for game, birds, vermin, etc. (For apparatus of fishing, see Group v).

Class 204.

Explosive and fulminating compounds, in small quantities only, and under special regulations; shown in the building only by empty cases and cartridges. Black powder of various grades and sizes. Nitro-glycerine and the methods of using and exploding. Giant powder, dynamite, dualin, tri-nitro-glycerine.

Class 205.

Pyrotechnics—for display, signaling, missiles, etc.

GROUP XVII.

CARRIAGES, VEHICLES, AND ACCESSORIES.

(For farm vehicles and railway carriages, etc., see Departments of Agriculture and Machinery.)

CLASS 292.

Pleasure carriages.

CLASS 293.

Traveling carriages, coaches, stages, omnibuses, hearses.

Bath chairs, velocipedes, baby carriages.

CLASS 294.

Vehicles for movement of goods and heavy objects, carts, wagons, trucks.

(For traction engines, see Group XVII).

CLASS 295.

Sleighs, sledges, sleds, etc.

CLASS 296.

Carriages and horse furniture, harness and saddlery, whips, spurs, horse-blankets, carriage robes, rugs, etc.

Parts of carriages—wheels, bodies, shafts, etc.

Springs, axles.

Carriage iron work and fittings.

Carriage hardware.

Carriage varnish, oil, lubricants, etc.

GROUP XVIII.

**RAILWAY PLANT, ROLLING STOCK, AND APPARATUS.
ROAD ENGINES.**

Class 570.

Locomotives, models, drawings, plans, etc.

Class 571.

Carriages, wagons, trucks, cars, etc.
Snow-plows.

Class 572.

Brakes, buffers, couplings.

Class 573.

Wheels, tires, axles, bearings, springs, etc.

Class 574.

Permanent way, ties, chairs, switches, etc.

Class 575.

Station arrangements, water-cranes, turn-tables.
Railway signals.

Class 576.

Miscellaneous locomotive attachments.

Class 577.

Street railways and cars.
Road and traction engines, etc.

GROUP XIX.

VESSELS AND APPARATUS OF TRANSPORTATION.

(*Not included in other groups.*)

CLASS 590.

Suspended-cable railways.

CLASS 591.

Transporting cables.

CLASS 592.

Balloons, and apparatus, etc.

CLASS 593.

See Group xx.

CLASS 594.

Boats and sailing vessels. Sailing vessels used in commerce. Sailing vessels used in war. Yachts and pleasure boats. Rowing boats of all kinds.

Life boats and salvage apparatus, with life rafts, belts, etc. Submarine armor, diving bells, etc. Ice boats.

CLASS 595.

Steamships, steamboats, and all vessels propelled by steam.

CLASS 554.

Screw propellers, wheels for the propulsion of vessels, etc.

Classification.

Class 596.

Vessels for carrying telegraph cables, and railway trains; also coal barges, water boats, and dredging-machines, screw and floating-docks ; and for other special purposes.

Class 597.

Steam capstans, windlasses, deck-winches, and steering apparatus.

Class 287.

Ropes, cordage.

GROUP XX.

MOTORS, HYDRAULIC AND PNEUMATIC APPARATUS, ETC.

CLASS 550.

Boilers and all steam or gas-generating apparatus for motive purposes.

CLASS 551.

Water-wheels, wind-mills.

CLASS 552.

Steam, air, or gas engines.
(For electro-magnetic engines, see Group XXV.)

CLASS 553.

Apparatus for the transmission of power, shafting, belting, cables, gearing; transmission of power by compressed air, etc.

CLASS 554.

(See Group XIX.)

CLASS 555.

Implements and apparatus used in connection with motors; steam-guages, manometers, etc. (See also Group XXV.)

CLASS 560.

Pumps and apparatus for lifting and moving liquids—water engines, hydraulic rams. (Class 551, in part.)

CLASS 561.

Pumps and apparatus for moving and compressing air or gas.

Class 562.

Pumps and blowing engines, blowers, and ventilating apparatus.

Class 563.

Pneumatic railways; pneumatic dispatch.

Class 563.

Hydraulic jacks, presses, elevators, lifts, cranes.
(For " meters" see Group xxv.)

Class 564.

Fire engines—hand, steam, or chemical; and fire extinguishing apparatus—hose, ladders, fire-escapes, etc.

Class 565.

Beer engines, soda-water machines, bottling apparatus, corking machines.

Class 566.

Stop valves, cocks, pipes, etc.

Class 567.

Diving apparatus and machinery.

Class 568.

Ice machines.

GROUP XXI.

MACHINE TOOLS.—WOOD, METAL AND STONE.

Class 510.

Planing, sawing, veneering, grooving, mortising, tonguing, cutting, moulding, stamping, carving, and cask-making machines, etc., cork-cutting machines.

Class 511.

Direct acting steam sawing machines, with gang saws.

Class 514.

Steam, trip, and other hammers, with specimens of work; anvils, forges.

Class 515.

Planing, drilling, slotting, turning, shaping, punching, stamping, and cutting machines. Wheel cutting and dividing machines.

Emery wheels and mountings.

Drills, taps, guages, dies, etc.

Class 516.

Stone-sawing and planing machines; machines for dressing, shaping, and polishing; sand blasts; Tilghman's machines; glass-grinding machines, etc.

GROUP XXII.

MACHINES, APPARATUS, AND IMPLEMENTS USED IN SEWING AND MAKING CLOTHING, LACE, ORNAMENTAL OBJECTS, PINS, Etc.

Class 530.

Machines used in the manufacture of tapestry, including carpets, lace, floor-cloth, fancy embroidery etc.

Class 531.

Sewing and knitting machines ; clothes making machines.

Class 534.

Machines for ironing, drying, and scouring.

Class 535.

Machines for making clocks and watches.

Class 536.

Machines for making jewelry.

Class 537.

Machines for making buttons, pins, needles, etc., and for sticking pins upon paper.

GROUP XXIII.

AGRICULTURAL MACHINES, IMPLEMENTS OF AGRICULTURE, HORTICULTURE AND GARDENING.

Class 607.—Tillage.

Manual Implements—spades, hoes, rakes. Animal power machinery—plows, cultivators, horse-hoes, clod crushers, rollers, harrows. Steam power machinery—plows, breakers, harrows, cultivators.

Class 671.—Planting.

Manual Implements—corn-planters and hand drills. Animal power machinery—grain and manure drills; corn and cotton planters. Steam power machinery—grain and manure drills.

Class 672.—Harvesting.

Manual implements—grain-cradles, sickles, reaping hooks. Animal power machinery—reapers and headers. Mowers, tedders, rakes, hay elevators, and hay loaders. Potato diggers.

Class 673.—Preparatory to Marketing.

Thrashers, clove-hullers, corn-shellers, winnowers, hay-making apparatus.

Class 674.—Applicable to Farm Economy.

Portable and stationary engines, chaffers, hay and feed-cutters, slicers, pulpers, corn mills, farm boilers and steamers, incubators. Churns for hand and power, butter-workers, cans and pails, cheese-presses, vats, and apparatus.

Class 680.—Laying Out and Improving Farms.

Clearing, stump-extractors, construction of roads, draining, irrigating apparatus, models of fences, gates, drains, out-falls, dams, embankments, irrigating machinery, stack building and thatching.

Class 681.—Commercial Fertilizers.

Phosphatic, ammoniacal. calcareous, etc.

Class 682.—Transportation.

Wagons, carts, sleds, harness. (See also Group XXVII). Yokes, and apparatus for road making and excavating. (For traction engines, see Group XVIII).

Class 683.—Farm Buildings.

Models and drawings of farm houses and tenements, barns, stables, hop-houses, fruit-driers, ice-houses, wind-mills, granaries, barracks, apiaries, cocooneries, aviaries, abattoirs, and dairies.

TILLAGE AND GENERAL MANAGEMENT.

Class 690.

Systems of planting and cultivation.

Class 691.

Systems of draining and application of manures.

Class 692.

Systems of breeding and stock feeding.

Class 715.

Horticultural buildings, propagating houses, hot-beds, etc., and modes of heating them. Structures for propagating and forcing small fruits.

CLASS 716.

Portable or movable orchard houses and graperies without artificial heat.

CLASS 675.

Dairy fittings and appliances.

GARDEN TOOLS, ACCESSORIES OF GARDENING.

CLASS 720.—TOOLS AND IMPLEMENTS.

Machines for the transplanting of trees, shrubs, etc. Portable forcing pumps, for watering plants in green houses, and methods of watering the garden and lawn.

CLASS 721.—RECEPTACLES FOR PLANTS.

Flower pots, plant-boxes, tubs, fern cases, jardinieres, etc. Window gardening. Plant and flower stands, ornate designs in iron, wood, and wire.

CLASS 722.—ORNAMENTAL WIRE WORK.

Fences, gates, trellis, bordering of flower beds, porches. Park seats, chairs, garden statuary, vases, fountains, etc. Designations, labels, numbers.

GARDEN DESIGNING. CONSTRUCTION, AND MANAGEMENT.

CLASS 710.—LAYING OUT GARDENS.

Designs for the laying out of gardens, and the improving of private residences. Designs for commercial gardens, nurseries, graperies. Designs for the parterre.

CLASS 731.

Treatment of water for ornamental purposes, cascades, fountains reservoirs, lakes.

Class 732.

Formation and after treatment of lawns.

Class 733.

Garden construction, buildings, etc. Rock work, grottoes.

Rustic constructions and adornments for private gardens and public grounds.

GROUP XXIV.

INSTRUMENTS AND APPARATUS OF HYGEINE, MEDICINE, SURGERY, PROSTHESIS, ETC.

Class 272.

Medicines, officinal, (in any authoritative pharmacopæ); articles of the materia medica; preparations, unofficinal.

Class 273.

Dietetic preparations, as beef extract, and other articles intended especially for the sick.

Class 275.

Instruments for physical diagnosis, clinical thermometers, stethoscopes, opthalmoscopes, etc., (except clinical microscopes, etc., for which see Class 324.)

Class 276.

Surgical instruments and appliances, with dressings, apparatus for deformities, prosthesis, obstetrical instruments.

Class 277.

Dental instruments appliances and materials.

Class 278.

Vehicles and appliances, for the transportation and relief of the sick and wounded, during peace and war, on shore or at sea.

GROUP XXV.

INSTRUMENTS OF PRECISION, RESEARCH, EXPERIMENT, AND ILLUSTRATION, INCLUDING TELEGRAPHY AND MUSIC.

CLASS 320.—ASTRONOMICAL, SURVEYING AND LEVELING INSTRUMENTS.

Astronomical instruments, and accessories, used in observatories.

Transits, mural circles, equatorials, collimators.

Geodetic and surveying instruments. Transits, theodolites, needle compasses. Instruments for surveying underground in mines, tunnels, and excavations.

Nautical astronomical instruments. Sextants, quadrants, repeating circles, dip-sectors.

Leveling instruments and apparatus. Carpenters' and builders' levels, hand levels, water levels, engineers' levels.

Instruments for deep sea sounding and hydrographic surveying.

METEOROLOGICAL INSTRUMENTS AND APPARATUS.

Thermometers, pyrometers.

Barometers.

Hygrometers and rain guages.

Maps, bulletins.

Blanks for reports, methods of recording, reducing, and reporting observations.

CLASS 321.

Indicating and registering apparatus, other than meteorological; mechanical calculation. (See also Group xx.)

Viameters, pedometers, perambulators.

Gas meters.

Water meters, current meters, ships' logs, electrical logs.

Tide registers.

Apparatus for printing consecutive numbers.

Counting machines, calculating engines, arithmometers.

CLASS 322.—WEIGHTS, MEASURES, WEIGHING AND METROLOGICAL APPARATUS.

Measures of length; graduated scales on wood, metal, ivory, tape, or ribbon; steel tapes, chains, rods, verniers, rods and graduated scales, for measuring lumber, goods in packages, casks, etc., guagers' tools and methods.

Measures of capacity for solids and liquids.

Weights. Scales and graduated beams for weighing; assay balances, chemical balances Ordinary scales for heavy weights, weighing locomotives and trains of cars. Postal balances. Hydrometers, alchometers, lactometers, etc., gravimeters.

CLASS 323.—CHRONOMETRIC APPARATUS.

Chronometers. Astronomical clocks. Church and metropolitan clocks. Ordinary commercial clocks. Pendulum and spring clocks. Marine clocks. Watches. Clepsydras, hour glasses, sun dials. Chronographs, electrical clocks. Metronomes.

CLASS 324.—OPTICAL AND THERMOTIC INSTRUMENTS, AND APPARATUS.

Mirrors (for special purposes), plane and spherical.

Lenses and prisms.

Spectacles and eye glasses, field and opera glasses, graphoscopes and stereoscopes.

Cameras and photographic apparatus.

Microscopes.

Telescopes. (See also Class 320.)

Apparatus for artificial illumination, including electric, oxy-hydrogen and magnesium light.

Stereopticons.

Photometric apparatus.

Spectroscopes and accessories, for spectrum analysis.

Polariscopes, etc.

Thermotic apparatus. Thermometers of all descriptions, maximum, minimum, self-registering, etc.

Class 325.—Electrical Apparatus.

Friction machines.

Condensers and miscellaneous apparatus, to illustrate the discharge.

Galvanic batteries and accessories, to illustrate dynamical electricity.

Electro-magnetic apparatus. Electro-magnetic engines, (See Class 552.)

Induction machines, Rumkoff coils, etc.

Magnets and magneto-electrical apparatus.

Class 326.

Telegraphic Instruments and Methods.

Batteries and forms of apparatus, used in generating the electrical currents for telegraphic purposes.

Conductors and insulators, and methods of support; marine telegraph cables.

Apparatus of transmission—keys, office accessories, and apparatus.

Receiving instruments, relay magnets, local circuits.

Semaphoric and recording instruments.

Codes, signs, or signals.

Printing telegraphs, for special uses.

Electrographs.

Dial or cadran systems.

Apparatus for automatic transmission.

CLASS 327.—MUSICAL INSTRUMENTS, AND ACOUSTICS, APPARATUS.
Percussion instruments—drums, tamborines, cymbals, triangles.

Pianos.

Stringed instruments other than pianos.

Automatic musical instruments, music boxes.

Wind instruments of metal and wood.

Harmoniums.

Church organs and similar instruments.

Speaking machines.

Vocal music.

GROUP XXVI.

ARCHITECTURE AND ENGINEERING.

(*For Agricultural Engineering, see Class 680*).
(*For Mine Engineering, See Group I*).

ARCHITECTURE.

The constrnction and arrangement of the interior of dwelling houses, hotels, public buildings, churches and buildings for special purposes. Fire-proof structures and methods of building.

CLASS 342.

The dwelling—sanitary conditions, and regulations.

Systems of water supply, drainage, heating, lighting, and ventilation. (For apparatus and fixtures see Group XIV).

CLASS 341.

Models and drawings of finished buildings, of market houses and markets, of hospitals, bath houses, gymnasiums, etc.

ENGINEERING.

CLASS 330.

CIVIL ENGINEERING.

Land surveying, public lands, etc.

River, harbor, and coast surveying. Construction and maintainance of roads, streets, pavements, etc. Surveys, and location of towns and cities, with systems of water supply and drainage. Arched bridges of metal, stone, brick, or beton. Trussed girder bridges. Suspension bridges, Canals, aqueducts, reservoirs; construction of dams. Hydraulic engineering, and means of arresting and controling the flow of water.

Submarine constructions, foundations, piers, docks, etc.

CLASS 331.—DYNAMIC AND INDUSTRIAL ENGINEERING.

Construction and working of machines; examples of planning, and construction of manufacturing and metallurgical establishments.

CLASS 332.— RAILWAY ENGINEERING.

Location of railways, and the construction and management of railways.

CLASS 333.—MILITARY ENGINEERING.

CLASS 335.—CHARTS, MAPS, AND GRAPHIC REPRESENTATIONS.

Topographical Maps Marine and coast charts.

Botanical, agronomical, and other maps, showing the extent and distribution of men, animals, and terrestrial products. Physical maps.

Meteorlogical maps and bulletins. Telegraphic routes and stations. Railway and route maps. Terrestrial and celestial globes. Relief maps and models of portions of the earth's surface. Profiles of ocean beds and routes of submarine cables.

GROUP XXVII.

PLASTIC AND GRAPHIC ART. SCULPTURE.

CLASS 400.

Figures and groups in stone, metal, clay or plaster.

CLASS 401.

Bas-relief, in stone or metal; electrotype copies.

CLASS 402.

Medals, pressed and engraved; electrotypes of medals.

CLASS 403.

Hammered and wrought work—*repoussé* and *rehausé* work: embossed and engraved relief work.

CLASS 404.

Cameos, intaglios, engraved stones, dies, seals, etc.

CLASS 405.

Carvings in wood, ivory, and metal.

PAINTING.

CTASS 410.

Painting in oil on canvas, panels etc.

Class 411.

Water color pictures; aquarelles, miniatures, etc.

Class 412.

Frescoes, cartoons for frescoes, etc.

Class 413.

Painting with vitrifiable colors. Pictures on porcelain, enamel, and metal.

ENGRAVING AND LITHOGRAPHY.

Class 420.

Drawings with pen, pencil or crayons.

Class 421.

Line engravings from steel, copper or stone.

Class 422.

Wood engravings.

Class 423.

Lithographs, zincographs, etc.

Class 424.

Chromo-lithographs.

PHOTOGRAPHY.

Class 430.

Photographs on paper, metal, glass, wood, fabrics or enamel surfaces, Micro-photographs.

CLASS 431.

Prints from photo-relief plates; carbon-prints, etc.

CLASS 432.

Photo-lithographs, etc.

INDUSTRIAL AND ARCHITECTURAL DESIGNS, MODELS, AND DECORATIONS.

CLASS 440.

Industrial designs.

CLASS 441.

Architectural designs : studies and fragments, representations and projects of edificies; restorations from ruins and from documents.

CLASS 442.

Decoration of interiors of building.

CLASS 443.

Artistic hardware and trimmings : artistic castings ; forged metal work for decoration, etc.

DECORATION WITH CERAMIC AND VITREOUS MATERIALS; MOSAIC AND INLAID WORK.

CLASS 450.

Mosaic and inlaid work in stone.

CLASS 451.

Mosaic and inlaid work in tiies, tesseræ, glass, etc.

Class 452.

Inlaid work in wood and metal; parquetry, inlaid floors, tables, etc.

Class 453.

Stained glass.

Class 454.

Miscellaneous objects of art.

GROUP XXVIII.

EDUCATION AND SCIENCE.

EDUCATIONAL SYSTEMS, METHODS AND LIBRARIES.

CLASS 300.—ELEMENTARY INSTRUCTION.

Infant schools and kindergartens—arrangements, furniture, appliances, and modes of training.

Public schools, graded schools, buildings and grounds, equipments, courses of study, methods of instruction, text books, apparatus, including maps, charts, globes, etc., pupils' work including drawing and penmanship; provisions for physical training.

CLASS 301.—HIGHER EDUCATION.

Academies and high schools.

Colleges and universities. Buildings and grounds, libraries, museums of zoology; botany, mineralogy, art, and archeology; apparatus for illustration and research; mathematical, physical, chemical, and astronomical courses of study; text books, catalogues; libraries, and gymnasiums.

CLASS 302.

Professional schools—theology, law, medicine and surgery, dentistry, pharmacy, mining, engineering, agriculture and mechanical arts, art and design, military schools, naval schools, normal schools, commercial schools, music.

Buildings, text books, libraries, apparatus, methods, and other accessories for professional schools.

CLASS 303.

Institutions for instruction of the blind, deaf and dumb and the feeble-minded.

Class 304.

Education reports and statistics.
National Bureau of education. State, city and town systems.
College, university, and professional systems.

Class 305.

Libraries, history, reports, statistics, and catalogues.

Class 306.

School and text books, dictionaries, encyclopædias, gazetteers, directories, index volumes, bibliographies, catalogues, almanacs, special treatises, general and miscellaneous literature.

Newspapers— technical and special newspapers and journals, illustrated papers, periodical literature.

INSTITUTIONS AND ORGANIZATIONS.

Class 310.

Institutions founded for the increase and diffusion of knowledge. Such as the Smithsonian Institution, the Royal Institution, the Institute of France, British Association for the Advancement of Science, and the American Association, etc., their organization, history, and results.

Class 311.

Learned and scientific associations. Geological and mineralogical societies, etc, Engineering, technical and professional associations artistic, biological. zoological, medical schools; astronomical observatories.

Class 312.

Museums, collections, art galleries, exhibitions of w rks of art and industry. Agricultural fairs, state und county exhibitions. national exhibitions. International exhibitions.

Scientific museums, and art museums.
Ethnological and archeological collections.

Class 313.

Music and the drama.

Printed in Dunstable, United Kingdom